Top 10 of the World

Layout and production: Liber AB

Editing: Alistair Dinwiddie, Gunilla Jernselius

Picture credits:
Alistair Dinwiddie
Creatas
Digital Stock
Digital Vision
Getty Images
Image100
Imageshop
Leica Geosystems
Markus Klein from Mainhausen, Germany
Magnús Tumi Guðmundsson, Iceland
Photoalto
Photodisc
Reuber, Germany
Structurae, Germany
Theres Wiklund, Uppsala, Sweden
U.S. Geological Survey, USA

Illustrations:
Book Matrix, Datagraph System, India
Liber AB

Printing: Deaprinting, Novara, Italy 2007
First edition
1
ISBN 978-91-47-80820-5

© Liber AB, Stockholm 2007

Liber AB, 113 98 Stockholm
Sweden
Tel. +46 (0)8-690 90 00
www.liber.se

Data in this book does not always come from official source material. The accuracy of the data has been checked, but in the case of curiosity facts it has not always been possible to substantiate the accuracy.

TOP 10 of the WORLD

This book contains world records within various geographical fields; both things created by nature, e.g. islands, lakes and deserts, and things constructed by man, e.g. buildings, bridges and tunnels.

The book contains brief descriptions of things that are useful to know, but also other things that are perhaps not essential, but are still interesting.

If you want to know whether something particular is included, check on page 66.

If there is a word you don't understand, it may be explained in the **Explanations of words** on page 56. All the words underlined in the text are explained.

Hope you find it interesting and learn lots of new facts.

WHERE CAN I FIND?

About People

About Built Structures

About finding words

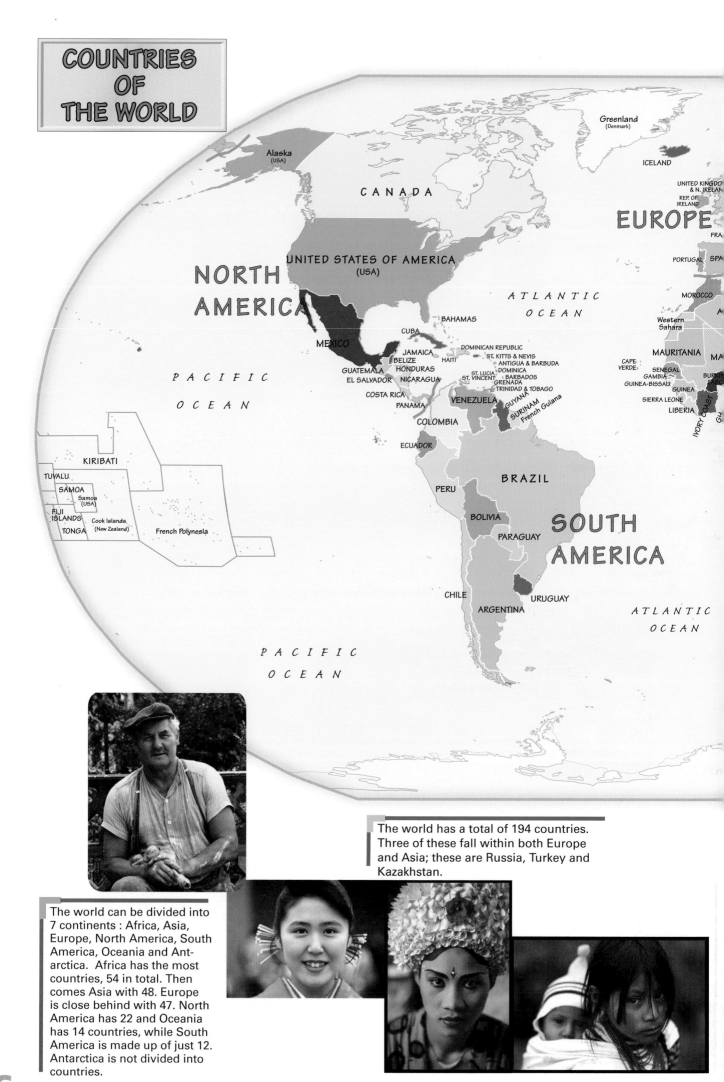

COUNTRIES OF THE WORLD

Greenland
(Denmark)

ICELAND

Alaska
(USA)

CANADA

UNITED KINGDO
& N. IRELAN
REP. OF
IRELAND

EUROPE

NORTH
AMERICA

UNITED STATES OF AMERICA
(USA)

ATLANTIC
OCEAN

PORTUGAL SPA

FRA

MOROCCO

MEXICO

PACIFIC

OCEAN

BAHAMAS

CUBA

DOMINICAN REPUBLIC

JAMAICA
BELIZE   HONDURAS
GUATEMALA
EL SALVADOR   NICARAGUA

HAITI

ST. KITTS & NEVIS
ANTIGUA & BARBUDA
DOMINICA
ST. LUCIA
ST. VINCENT   BARBADOS
GRENADA
TRINIDAD & TOBAGO

Western
Sahara

MAURITANIA

MA

CAPE
VERDE
SENEGAL
GAMBIA
GUINEA-BISSAU
GUINEA

BURKI
FASO

COSTA RICA

PANAMA

VENEZUELA

COLOMBIA

GUYANA
SURINAM
French Guiana

SIERRA LEONE

LIBERIA

GH

IVORY COAST

ECUADOR

KIRIBATI

TUVALU

SAMOA
Samoa
(USA)

FIJI
ISLANDS

TONGA

Cook Islands
(New Zealand)

French Polynesia

PERU

BRAZIL

BOLIVIA

PARAGUAY

SOUTH
AMERICA

PACIFIC

OCEAN

CHILE

ARGENTINA

URUGUAY

ATLANTIC
OCEAN

The world has a total of 194 countries.
Three of these fall within both Europe
and Asia; these are Russia, Turkey and
Kazakhstan.

The world can be divided into
7 continents : Africa, Asia,
Europe, North America, South
America, Oceania and Ant-
arctica. Africa has the most
countries, 54 in total. Then
comes Asia with 48. Europe
is close behind with 47. North
America has 22 and Oceania
has 14 countries, while South
America is made up of just 12.
Antarctica is not divided into
countries.

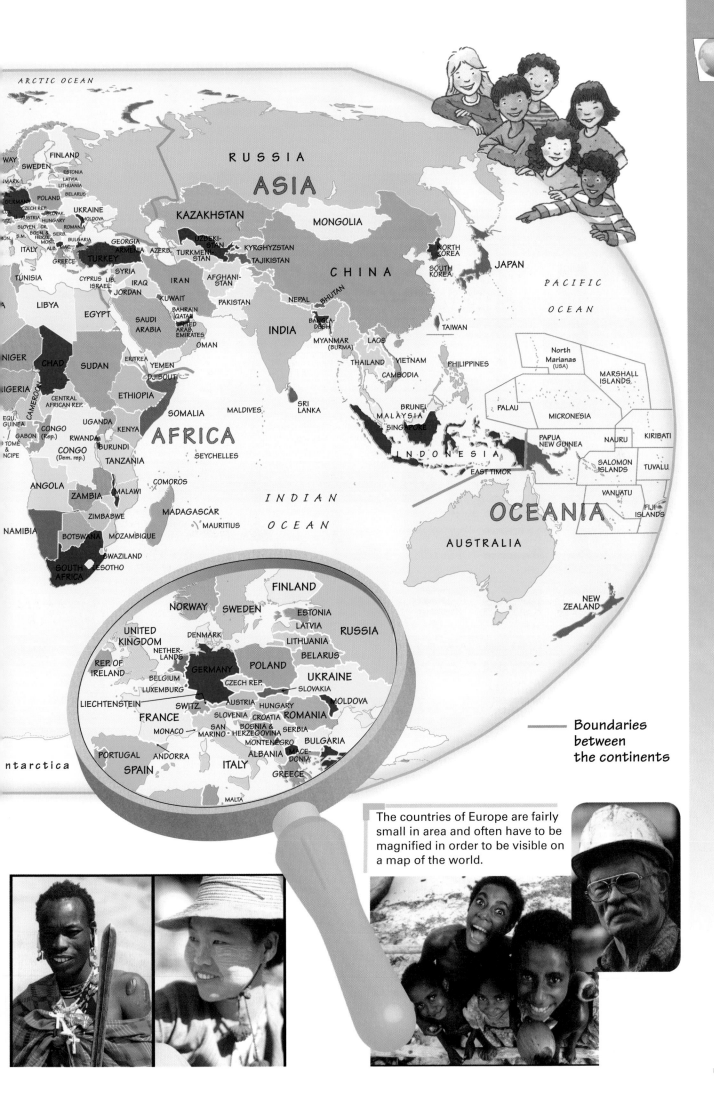

ARCTIC OCEAN

WAY
FINLAND
SWEDEN
MARK
GERMANY
POLAND
CZECH REP.
SLOVAK.
UKRAINE
AUSTRIA
HUNGARY
MOLDOVA
SLOVEN. CR.
ROMANIA
B.M.
BOSN. &
HERZEG.
SERB.
ITALY
MONT.
BULGARIA
ALB. MAC.
ION.
GREECE

ESTONIA
LATVIA
LITHUANIA
BELARUS

RUSSIA

ASIA

KAZAKHSTAN

MONGOLIA

GEORGIA
ARMENIA
AZERB.
UZBEKI-
STAN
TURKMENI-
STAN
KYRGHYZSTAN
TAJIKISTAN
TURKEY
SYRIA

NORTH
KOREA
SOUTH
KOREA
JAPAN

PACIFIC
OCEAN

TUNISIA
CYPRUS LIB.
ISRAEL
JORDAN
IRAQ
IRAN
AFGHANI-
STAN
CHINA

LIBYA
EGYPT
KUWAIT
BAHRAIN
QATAR
UNITED
ARAB.
EMIRATES
SAUDI
ARABIA
OMAN
PAKISTAN
NEPAL
BHUTAN
BANGLA-
DESH
INDIA
MYANMAR
(BURMA)
LAOS
TAIWAN

NIGER
CHAD
SUDAN
ERITREA
YEMEN
DJIBOUTI
THAILAND
VIETNAM
CAMBODIA
PHILIPPINES

NIGERIA
CAMEROON
CENTRAL
AFRICAN REP.
ETHIOPIA
SOMALIA
MALDIVES
SRI
LANKA
BRUNEI
MALAYSIA
SINGAPORE

EQU.
GUINEA
GABON
TOMÉ
&
NCIPE
CONGO
(Rep.)
UGANDA
RWANDA
KENYA
AFRICA
SEYCHELLES
INDONESIA
North
Marianas
(USA)
MARSHALL
ISLANDS
PALAU
MICRONESIA
KIRIBATI
NAURU

CONGO
(Dem. rep.)
BURUNDI
TANZANIA
EAST TIMOR
PAPUA
NEW GUINEA
SALOMON
ISLANDS
TUVALU

ANGOLA
ZAMBIA
MALAWI
COMOROS
INDIAN
OCEANIA
VANUATU

NAMIBIA
ZIMBABWE
MOZAMBIQUE
MADAGASCAR
MAURITIUS
OCEAN
AUSTRALIA
FIJI
ISLANDS

BOTSWANA
SWAZILAND
SOUTH
AFRICA
LESOTHO
NEW
ZEALAND

ntarctica

FINLAND
NORWAY
SWEDEN
ESTONIA
LATVIA
RUSSIA
UNITED
KINGDOM
DENMARK
LITHUANIA
NETHER-
LANDS
BELARUS
REP. OF
IRELAND
GERMANY
POLAND
BELGIUM
LUXEMBURG
CZECH REP.
UKRAINE
LIECHTENSTEIN
SLOVAKIA
SWITZ.
AUSTRIA
HUNGARY
MOLDOVA
FRANCE
SLOVENIA
CROATIA
ROMANIA
MONACO
SAN
MARINO
BOSNIA &
HERZEGOVINA
SERBIA
MONTENEGRO
BULGARIA
PORTUGAL
ANDORRA
ALBANIA
MACE-
DONIA
SPAIN
ITALY
GREECE
MALTA

——— Boundaries
between
the continents

The countries of Europe are fairly
small in area and often have to be
magnified in order to be visible on
a map of the world.

7

FLAGS OF EUROPE

 Norway
 Sweden
 Finland

 Faroe Islands
 Iceland
 Denmark
 Lithuania
 Latvia
 Estonia

 Ireland
 United Kingdom
 Belgium
 Netherlands
 Germany
 Poland
 Belarus

 Luxembourg
 Liechtenstein
 Austria
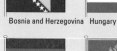 Czech Republic
 Slovakia
 Moldova
 Ukraine

 France
 Switzerland
 Slovenia
 Croatia
 Bosnia and Herzegovina
 Hungary
 Romania
 Bulgaria

 Monaco
 Italy
 Vatican City State
 San Marino
 Serbia
 Montenegro
 Albania
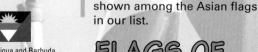 Macedonia

 Portugal
 Spain
 Andorra
 Malta
 Greece
 Cyprus

FLAGS OF NORTH & CENTRAL AMERICA

 Canada
United States
Greenland

Mexico
Belize
Cuba
Bahamas
Haiti
Dominican Republic

Guatemala
Honduras
Jamaica
Puerto Rico
Saint Kitts and Nevis
Antigua and Barbuda

El Salvador
Nicaragua
Dominica
Saint Lucia
Saint Vincent and the Grenadines
Barbados

Costa Rica
Panama
Grenada

Russia, Kazakhstan and Turkey - 3 nations that form part of 2 different continents. They have a smaller part of their land area in Europe and a larger part in Asia. These are shown among the Asian flags in our list.

FLAGS OF OCEANIA

 Palau
 Marshall Islands

 Micronesia
 Nauru

 Papua New Guinea
 Kiribati

 Solomon Islands
 Tuvalu

 Vanuatu
 Samoa

 Fiji Islands
 Tonga

 Australia
 New Zealand

FLAGS OF SOUTH AMERICA

Trinidad and Tobago

Colombia
Venezuela
Guyana
Suriname

Ecuador
Peru
Bolivia
Brazil

Chile
Argentina
Paraguay
Uruguay

FLAGS OF AFRICA

Cape Verde
Mauritania
Western Sahara
Morocco
Algeria
Tunisia
Libya
Egypt
Senegal
The Gambia
Mali
Niger
Chad
Sudan
Ethiopia
Eritrea
Guinea-Bissau
Guinea
Sierra Leone
Burkina Faso
Nigeria
Cameroon
Central Africa
Djibouti
Liberia
Cote d'Ivoire
Ghana
Togo
Benin
Uganda
Kenya
Somalia
São Tomé and Príncipe
Equatorial Guinea
Gabon
Congo (Rep.)
Congo (Dem. Rep.)
Rwanda
Burundi
Tanzania
Angola
Zambia
Malawi
Comoros
Seychelles
Madagascar
Mauritius
Namibia
Botswana
Zimbabwe
Mozambique

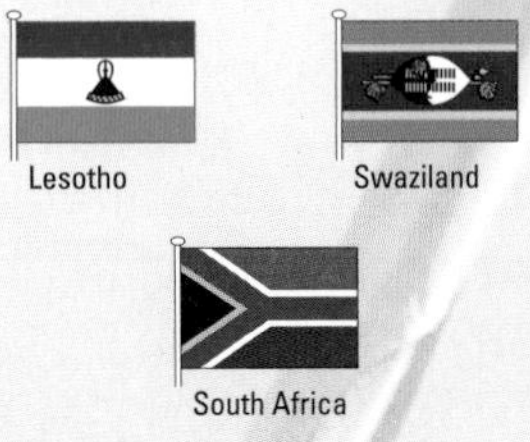

Lesotho
Swaziland
South Africa

The first people to use flags as a **symbol** of their nation were the small republics of Genoa and Venice, in the 1200s. During the geographic **voyages of discovery** in the 1500s, flags began to be used at sea. In the 1600s, **naval flags** began to be used to discourage pirates.

National flags have not always been used. During the French Revolution in 1789, the French Tricolour (three colours) was created as a symbol of freedom. General use of flags became common around 1900.

Some of the flags shown here are for areas that are part of another country but are striving for greater autonomy.

FLAGS OF ASIA

Kazakhstan
Russia
Mongolia

East Timor has been an **independent** nation since 2002 and now has its own flag.

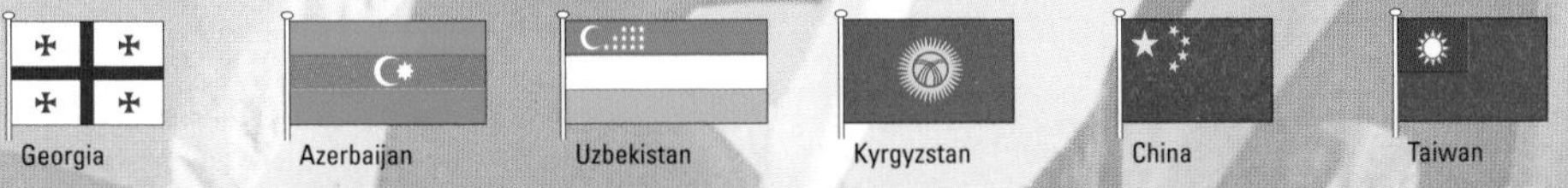

Georgia
Azerbaijan
Uzbekistan
Kyrgyzstan
China
Taiwan

Turkey
Armenia
Turkmenistan
Tajikistan
Nepal
North Korea
South Korea
Japan
Lebanon
Syria
Iraq
Iran
Afghanistan
Pakistan
India
Bhutan
Israel
Palestine
Jordan
Kuwait
Bangladesh
Myanmar (Burma)
Laos
Vietnam
Saudi Arabia
Bahrain
Qatar
United Arab Emirates
Sri Lanka
Thailand
Cambodia
Philippines
Yemen
Oman
Maldives
Malaysia
Singapore
Brunei
Indonesia
East Timor

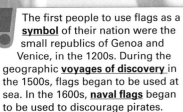

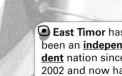

The highest MOUNTAINS

1	**Mount Everest**	Nepal	8,850 m
2	**Mount Godwin Austen**	Pakistan	8,610 m
3	**Kangchenjunga**	India	8,538 m
4	**Lhotse 1**	China	8,516 m
5	**Makalu**	China	8,481 m
6	**Cho Oyu**	China	8,201 m
7	**Dhaulagiri**	Nepal	8,172 m
8	**Nanga Parbat**	Nepal	8,126 m
9	**Manaslu**	Pakistan	8,124 m
10	**Annapurna**	Nepal	8,078 m

m = metres above sea level

The highest mountain on each continent

Mount Everest	Asia	8,850 m
Aconcagua	South America	6,960 m
Mount McKinley	North America	6,193 m
Kilimanjaro	Africa	5,892 m
Elbrus	Europe	5,642 m
Mount Wilhelm	Oceania	4,580 m

Did you know . . . ?

... that some people believe an abominable snowman, **yeti**, lives in the Himalayas.

... that the air at high altitudes contains less **oxygen**, so it's more difficult to breathe.

... that the snow leopard lives in the Central Asian **mountain ranges** and is very **rare**.

... that the Earth's surface consists of various plates that move. When they collide, **mountain ranges** are formed.

... that **llamas** have adapted to living at altitudes of 4,000 metres, where the air is low in **oxygen**.

... that the **radius** of the Earth is 700 times greater than the height of Mount Everest.

Mount McKinley in Alaska is North America's highest mountain. It was first climbed in 1913 and is named after an American **president**, William McKinley.

Mount McKinley

Rocky Mountains

NORTH AMERICA

Hawaii's **volcano Mauna Kea** is actually the world's highest mountain if you measure from the ocean floor to its summit. This makes it 10,069 metres high.

Andes

SOUTH AMERICA

Aconcagua is the western **hemisphere's** highest mountain. It is located in the world's longest **mountain range**, the Andes, and was first climbed in 1897 by Mathias Zurbriggen from Switzerland.

Aconcagua

High mountains

Mt. Everest
8,850 m

Aconcagua
6,960 m

Mt. Godwin Austen (K2)
8,610 m

Mt. McKinley
6,193 m

Kilimanjaro
5,892 m

Puncak Jaya
5,030 m

Matterhorn
4,478 m

Mt. Fuji
3,776 m

Mt. Blanc
4,810 m

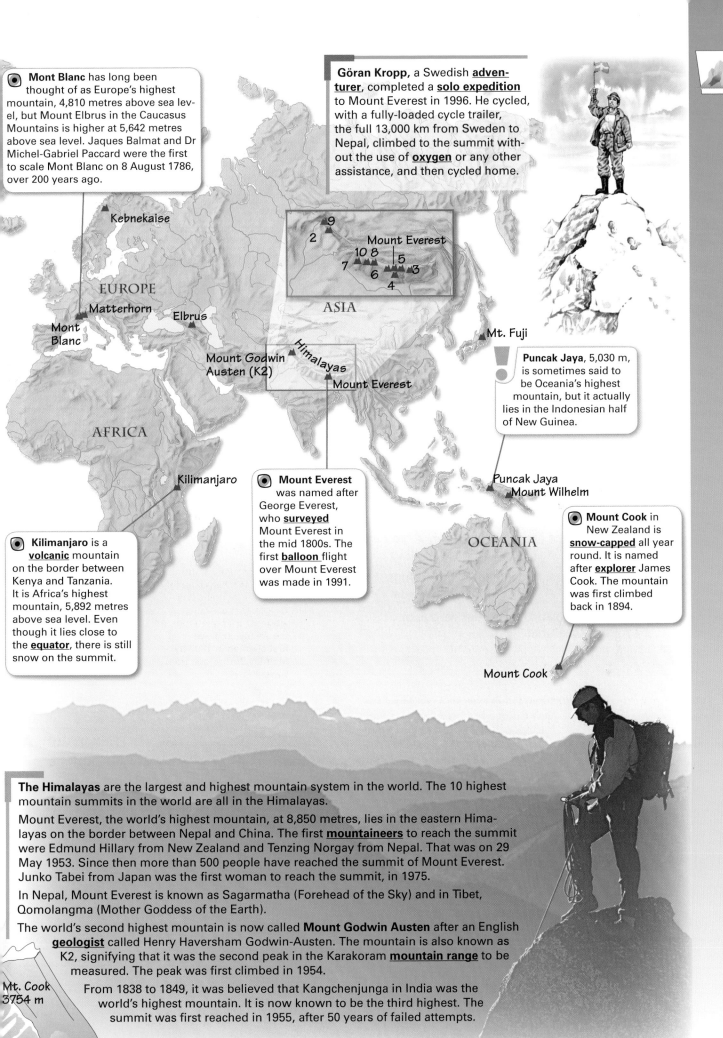

Mont Blanc has long been thought of as Europe's highest mountain, 4,810 metres above sea level, but Mount Elbrus in the Caucasus Mountains is higher at 5,642 metres above sea level. Jaques Balmat and Dr Michel-Gabriel Paccard were the first to scale Mont Blanc on 8 August 1786, over 200 years ago.

Göran Kropp, a Swedish **adventurer**, completed a **solo expedition** to Mount Everest in 1996. He cycled, with a fully-loaded cycle trailer, the full 13,000 km from Sweden to Nepal, climbed to the summit without the use of **oxygen** or any other assistance, and then cycled home.

Kebnekaise

9

2

Mount Everest

10 8

7   5

6   3

4

EUROPE

ASIA

Matterhorn

Mont Blanc

Elbrus

Mt. Fuji

Mount Godwin Austen (K2)

Himalayas

Mount Everest

Puncak Jaya, 5,030 m, is sometimes said to be Oceania's highest mountain, but it actually lies in the Indonesian half of New Guinea.

AFRICA

Kilimanjaro

Mount Everest was named after George Everest, who **surveyed** Mount Everest in the mid 1800s. The first **balloon** flight over Mount Everest was made in 1991.

Puncak Jaya
Mount Wilhelm

OCEANIA

Mount Cook in New Zealand is **snow-capped** all year round. It is named after **explorer** James Cook. The mountain was first climbed back in 1894.

Kilimanjaro is a **volcanic** mountain on the border between Kenya and Tanzania. It is Africa's highest mountain, 5,892 metres above sea level. Even though it lies close to the **equator**, there is still snow on the summit.

Mount Cook

Mt. Cook
3754 m

The Himalayas are the largest and highest mountain system in the world. The 10 highest mountain summits in the world are all in the Himalayas.

Mount Everest, the world's highest mountain, at 8,850 metres, lies in the eastern Himalayas on the border between Nepal and China. The first **mountaineers** to reach the summit were Edmund Hillary from New Zealand and Tenzing Norgay from Nepal. That was on 29 May 1953. Since then more than 500 people have reached the summit of Mount Everest. Junko Tabei from Japan was the first woman to reach the summit, in 1975.

In Nepal, Mount Everest is known as Sagarmatha (Forehead of the Sky) and in Tibet, Qomolangma (Mother Goddess of the Earth).

The world's second highest mountain is now called **Mount Godwin Austen** after an English **geologist** called Henry Haversham Godwin-Austen. The mountain is also known as K2, signifying that it was the second peak in the Karakoram **mountain range** to be measured. The peak was first climbed in 1954.

From 1838 to 1849, it was believed that Kangchenjunga in India was the world's highest mountain. It is now known to be the third highest. The summit was first reached in 1955, after 50 years of failed attempts.

The Largest ISLANDS

#	Island	Region
1	Greenland	North America
2	New Guinea	Asia-Oceania
3	Borneo	Asia
4	Madagascar	Africa
5	Baffin Is.	North America
6	Sumatra	Asia
7	Honshu	Asia
8	Victoria Is.	North America
9	Great Britain	Europe
10	Ellesmere Is.	North America

◉ Cape Columbia on **Ellesmere Island** is Canada's most northerly point. The island is home to herds of **musk oxen**.

Greenland, the largest island in the world, belongs to Denmark, but forms part of the **continent** of North America. The Greenlandic name for the island is **Kalaallit Nunaat**, "Land of the Greenlanders". The **capital** is called Nuuk and has 15,000 inhabitants. The people living in Greenland are **Inuit**, but are also known as **Eskimos**.

◉ **Victoria Island** in northern Canada is dominated by tundra. It has a **weather station**, but not many people live on this **Arctic** island.

◉ **Baffin Island** belongs to the **territory** of Nunavut in Canada. The capital of the island is called Iqaluit.

Victoria Island

Ellesmere Island

Greenland

Baffin Island

NORTH AMERICA

SOUTH AMERICA

Did you know . . . ?

... that the largest river island in the world is Bananal Island in Brazil.

... that the words "**anorak**" and "**parka**" come from the Greenlandic names for such jackets.

... that the largest lake island in the world is Manitoulin Island in Lake Huron in Canada.

... that New Zealand has no dangerous or poisonous creatures.

New Guinea lies between Asia and Australia. The western half of the island belongs to Indonesia, while the eastern half is a separate country, **Papua New Guinea**.

The word papua comes from Malay and means "curly-headed".

Borneo is roughly as large as Sweden and Norway together. Borneo is called Kalimantan in Indonesian.

Orang utans are now only found on Borneo and on Sumatra. The word orang utan means "person of the forest". Orang utans live high up in the trees in the **tropical rainforest** and are skilled at climbing.

Borneo
755,000 km²

Baffin Island
507,451 km²

Greenland
2,200,000 km²

New Guinea
785,000 km²

Madagascar
587,000 km²

Sumatra
425,000 km²

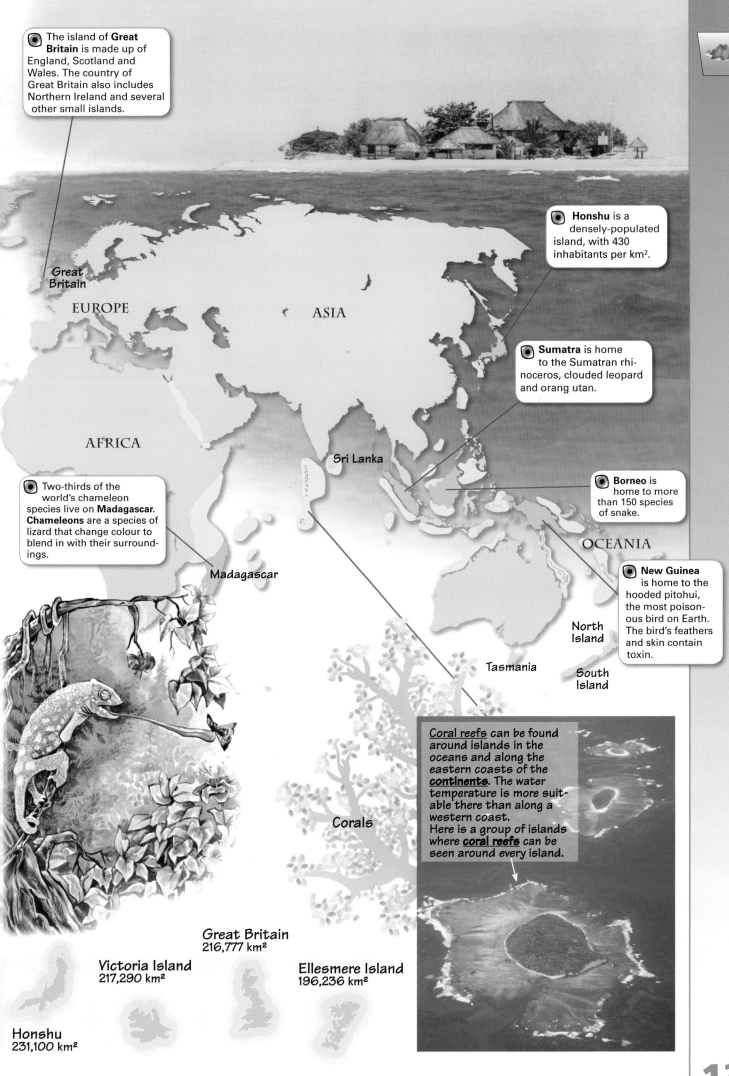

The island of **Great Britain** is made up of England, Scotland and Wales. The country of Great Britain also includes Northern Ireland and several other small islands.

Honshu is a densely-populated island, with 430 inhabitants per km².

Sumatra is home to the Sumatran rhinoceros, clouded leopard and orang utan.

Two-thirds of the world's chameleon species live on **Madagascar**. **Chameleons** are a species of lizard that change colour to blend in with their surroundings.

Borneo is home to more than 150 species of snake.

New Guinea is home to the hooded pitohui, the most poisonous bird on Earth. The bird's feathers and skin contain toxin.

Great Britain

EUROPE

ASIA

AFRICA

Sri Lanka

Madagascar

OCEANIA

North Island

Tasmania

South Island

Corals

Coral reefs can be found around islands in the oceans and along the eastern coasts of the **continents**. The water temperature is more suitable there than along a western coast.
Here is a group of islands where **coral reefs** can be seen around every island.

Great Britain
216,777 km²

Victoria Island
217,290 km²

Ellesmere Island
196,236 km²

Honshu
231,100 km²

FORESTS
of the World

Large parts of North America and Europe were once covered by vast forests. Natural **coniferous forests** are only left now in a few areas. If you want to visit undisturbed forest, you have to go to really inaccessible parts of the world.

Large areas of the **tropical forests** around the **equator** have been chopped down by humans. This affects the animals and plants that live there. Many of the Earth's flowering herbs and trees come from these parts of the world.

Coniferous forests are largely found in the northern **hemisphere** in North America, Europe and Asia. They mostly consist of spruce and pine. Bears, elk and lynx live in coniferous forests.

NORTH AMERICA

California

Nevada

Oldest

The oldest known tree is a pine in Nevada that lived to 5,100 years old.

Largest

The largest tree in the world is a **giant sequoia** in California. It is known as General Sherman and is 31.3 metres around the circumference of its trunk.

The agouti is a small animal that lives in the rainforest.

agouti = dasyproct

Equator

Amazon rainforest

SOUTH AMERICA

⊙ The oldest tree still living is a **bristlecone pine** in California which is 4,733 years old. It is known as Methuselah.

⊙ The **Redwood** is the **tallest tree species** in the world. The tallest individual tree is called Hyperion. It is 115.5 metres tall and can be found in California.

Trees are a plant with a woody stem. **Forests** consist of areas with trees that are tall and stand close together. Forests can be divided into different types.

Deciduous forest consists of hardwood trees such as oak, beech, elm, lime and maple. You can find roe deer, wild boar and squirrels in deciduous forests.

In **mixed forest** you often find birch and larch. Animals such as foxes and red deer thrive here.

Did you know . . . ?

... that the Dyerville Giant, once the biggest tree in the world, fell in a storm in 1991.

... that **bonsai** means "tray planting" and involves very small trees of various species.

... that there is a **prehistoric** tree species still living, the **ginkgo**.

... that a fully-grown tree consumes 70 litres of water on a hot summer day.

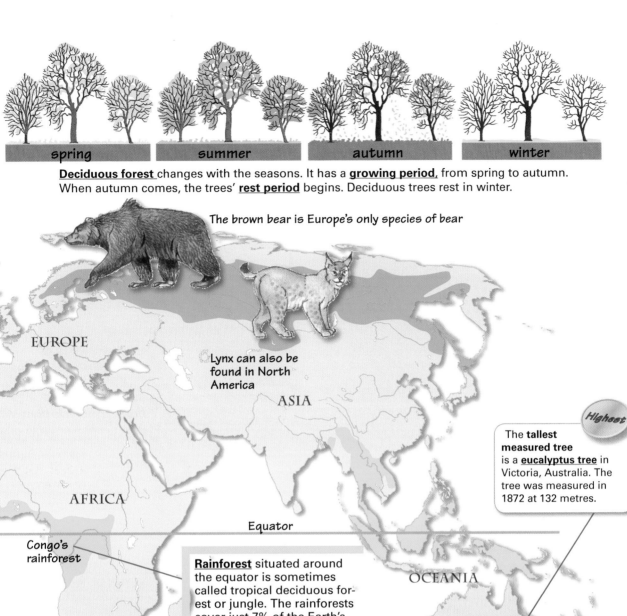

Deciduous forest changes with the seasons. It has a growing period, from spring to autumn. When autumn comes, the trees' rest period begins. Deciduous trees rest in winter.

The brown bear is Europe's only species of bear

EUROPE

Lynx can also be found in North America

ASIA

AFRICA

Equator

Congo's rainforest

OCEANIA

Australia

Tasmania

Highest

The **tallest measured tree** is a **eucalyptus tree** in Victoria, Australia. The tree was measured in 1872 at 132 metres.

Rainforest situated around the equator is sometimes called tropical deciduous forest or jungle. The rainforests cover just 7% of the Earth's surface, but contain many more species than the rest of the world. The size of the rainforests is decreasing due to **logging,** and the forests are threatened.

⊙ A eucalyptus tree in the Styx Valley on Tasmania is the tallest living deciduous tree in the world, 110 metres.

Rainy season

Dry season

Monsoon forests can be found in southern and south-western parts of Asia. Monsoon forests grow in a belt round the **equator** and have an intensive rainy season. After that comes the **dry season,** when most of the trees lose their leaves.

Rainforests south of the **equator** have a lot of rain throughout the year. Everything grows very rapidly, and it quickly becomes a dense **jungle** with large plants. The forest around the Amazon River is a **rainforest**.

15

The Largest DESERTS

1	Sahara Desert	Africa
2	Australian Desert	Oceania
3	Arabian Desert	Asia
4	Karakum Desert	Asia
5	North American Desert	North America
6	Patagonian Desert	South America
7	Kalahari Desert	Africa
8	Thar Desert	Asia
9	Taklamakan	Asia
10	Iranian Desert	Asia

The Sahara extends 5,000 kilometres, all the way from the Atlantic to the Red Sea. It contains **stony deserts**, **rock deserts** and **sand deserts**. Under the sand there are oil and gas that are **transported** via **pipelines** to the coast.

The Sahara is home to the **Tuareg**. They are a people who live as **nomads** and camel-herders. Their wound **turban** protects against sand and sun.

NORTH AMERICA

Death Valley

● Part of the **North American Desert** is known as **Death Valley** because it is so dry and hot. It lies 86 metres below sea level, and is the lowest point in North America. The rattlesnake is a typical desert creature there.

Mammals that live in the desert are mostly **nocturnal**. They burrow under ground during the day to escape the heat and avoid becoming prey for other **predators**.

The **fennec** has large ears and, consequently, can hear extremely well. Thanks to its excellent hearing, it can easily hunt at night.

The body of the **kangaroo rat** is such that it does not have much contact with the hot sand.

Snakes are common in the desert, as they can move about more easily than **four-footed** creatures. They move rapidly between sun and shade.

SOUTH AMERICA

Atacama Desert

Patagonian Desert

● The **Patagonian Desert** is one of the driest deserts on Earth. There are many sheep farmers there.

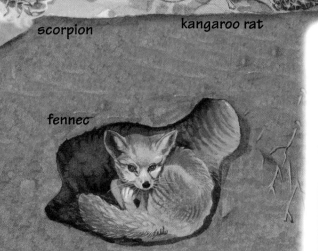

roadrunner

rattlesnake

scorpion

kangaroo rat

fennec

Did you know . . . ?

... that the **Atacama Desert** in Chile is the driest in the world, with just 12 mm **precipitation** per year.

... that you can experience **mirages** in the desert. You can believe that you see a lake, but it is just the air and heat making it look like a reflective surface.

... that there are **oases** in the middle of the desert. The **groundwater** comes up out of the ground so that plants and palms can grow.

... that camels are known as ships of the desert.

... that there are even deserts around the North and South Pole, because it snows so little.

Wind and sand

the wind blows — grains of sand drop down

sand dune

Sand dunes are formed when the wind forces sand up a rise in the sand.

Vortexes are created behind the crest and grains of sand drop down and form a steep side. At the same time the dunes move forward in the direction the wind is blowing. **Sand dunes** can be 30-100 metres high!

The **Arabian Desert** covers a large part of the Arabian Peninsula. More oil **extraction** takes place here than anywhere else in the world. Many **sheikhs** have become rich through selling oil.

Karakum, which means black sand, is a desert region in Turkmenistan. A canal constructed through the desert to irrigate **cotton plantations** is contributing to reducing the water level of the Aral Sea.

The **Taklamakan** is a large **sand desert** in China. Swede Sven Hedin made several journeys and **expeditions** through the deserts of Asia between 1894 and 1909.

EUROPE

ASIA

Aral Sea

Karakum

Takla-makan

Gobi Desert

Sahara

Arabian Desert

Thar Desert

The **Thar Desert** in Pakistan and India is made up of **sand dunes** and bare rock. Some years it doesn't rain at all here.

AFRICA

Approximately 2 million people live in the **Sahara**. Around half a million of these are **Tuareg**.

OCEANIA

Namib Desert

Kalahari

Some children who live in parts of the **Australian Desert** have school lessons via **radio communication** because they live too far away from any school.

Australian Desert

The **Kalahari** in southern Africa is home to **Bushmen**, who were previously **nomads**, but most are now **settled**.

Camels are animals made for coping with drought and heat. They can go without water for two weeks. The single-hump camel, the **dromedary**, is most common in Africa.

The "Saguaro" species of cactus can grow up to 15 metres high and live to be 200 years old.

The Largest GLACIERS

1	**Antarctic Ice Sheet**	Antarctica
2	**Greenland Ice Sheet**	Greenland
3	**Austfonna and Vestfonna**	Svalbard
4	**Vatnajökull**	Island
5	**Bering Glacier**	Alaska
6	**Olav V Land**	Svalbard
7	**Patagonian Glaciers**	Chile
8	**Malaspina Glacier**	Alaska
9	**Novaja Zemlja Glacier**	Russia
10	**Nabesna Glacier**	Alaska

Did you know...?

... that **nunatak** is the term for a **peak of rock** sticking up out of **inland ice**.

... any **glacier** that borders a deep-water stretch of ocean loses large **blocks of ice**, which form floating **icebergs**.

No trees grow in Greenland because the ground is always frozen. The ice on Greenland is up to 3,500 metres thick.

The **Humboldt Glacier** in the north west is the largest glacier in Greenland. The glacier grows by approximately 30 cm a year from snow and ice, but some of it melts away too.

Did you know . . . ?

... that only 1/7 of an **iceberg** shows above the surface of the water. The rest is below the surface.

... that 10% of the Earth's land area is covered by **glaciers**.

... that there are even glaciers near the **equator**, on Kilimanjaro in Africa and in the Andes in South America.

The **Bering Glacier** in southern Alaska is the largest in North America. Near the Canadian border you will also find the Malaspina Glacier and the Nabesna Glacier.

Musk oxen are native to Canada and Greenland. A number of musk oxen were imported from Greenland to Dovrefjell in Norway at the beginning of the 1900s. Some also migrated over to Sweden in 1971.

The **Patagonian Glaciers** lie on the border between Chile and Argentina. A large number of Humboldt penguins previously lived on the west coast of South America.

How a glacier is formed!

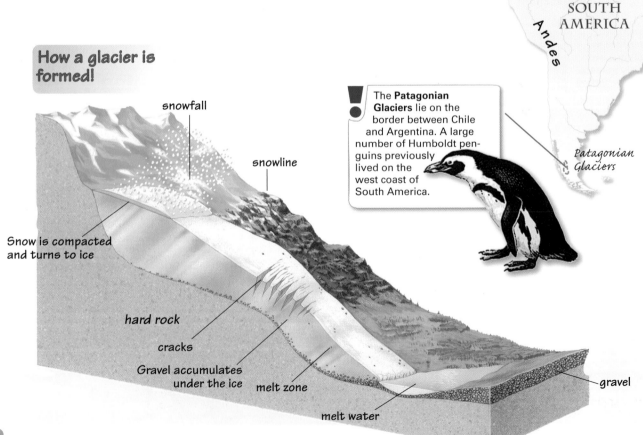

snowfall

snowline

Snow is compacted and turns to ice

hard rock

cracks

Gravel accumulates under the ice

melt zone

melt water

gravel

Humboldt Glacier

Nabesna Glacier

Bering Glacier

Malaspina Glacier

NORTH AMERICA

SOUTH AMERICA

Andes

Patagonian Glaciers

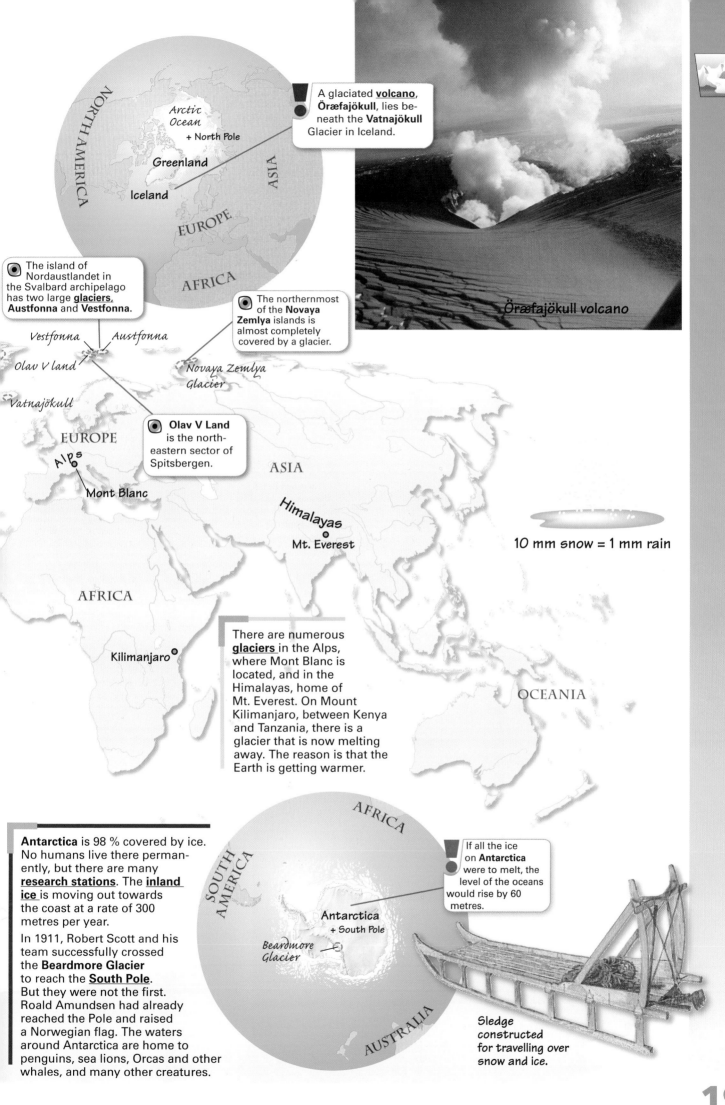

A glaciated **volcano**, **Öræfajökull**, lies beneath the **Vatnajökull** Glacier in Iceland.

Arctic Ocean
+ North Pole

NORTH AMERICA

Greenland

Iceland

ASIA

EUROPE

AFRICA

Öræfajökull volcano

The island of Nordaustlandet in the Svalbard archipelago has two large **glaciers**, **Austfonna** and **Vestfonna**.

The northernmost of the **Novaya Zemlya** islands is almost completely covered by a glacier.

Vestfonna   Austfonna

Olav V land

Novaya Zemlya Glacier

Vatnajökull

EUROPE

Alps

Mont Blanc

Olav V Land is the north-eastern sector of Spitsbergen.

ASIA

Himalayas
Mt. Everest

10 mm snow = 1 mm rain

AFRICA

Kilimanjaro

OCEANIA

There are numerous **glaciers** in the Alps, where Mont Blanc is located, and in the Himalayas, home of Mt. Everest. On Mount Kilimanjaro, between Kenya and Tanzania, there is a glacier that is now melting away. The reason is that the Earth is getting warmer.

AFRICA

Antarctica is 98 % covered by ice. No humans live there permanently, but there are many **research stations**. The **inland ice** is moving out towards the coast at a rate of 300 metres per year.

In 1911, Robert Scott and his team successfully crossed the **Beardmore Glacier** to reach the **South Pole**. But they were not the first. Roald Amundsen had already reached the Pole and raised a Norwegian flag. The waters around Antarctica are home to penguins, sea lions, Orcas and other whales, and many other creatures.

SOUTH AMERICA

Antarctica
+ South Pole

Beardmore Glacier

If all the ice on **Antarctica** were to melt, the level of the oceans would rise by 60 metres.

AUSTRALIA

Sledge constructed for travelling over snow and ice.

Global WEATHER

Weather describes the state of the water and air in the **atmosphere**. Weather is also precipitation, temperature, wind and cloudiness at a specific place and time.

Man has long tried to influence the weather. When the Indians danced their **rain dance**, it often rained the following day. It is now believed that the rainmakers, as they were known, had learned to tell from the sky when rain would come.

The temperature changed from +7 °C to -48 °C in a single 24-hour period in Browning, Montana, USA on 23 January 1916.

A snowflake that was 38 cm in diameter was recorded in Montana, USA in 1887.

Strongest

The **strongest wind-force** ever recorded on Earth is 333 km per hour. That was in 1972 in Thule, Greenland.

○ Thule

NORTH AMERICA
● Montana

Deepest

○ California

The **greatest depth of snow** ever recorded was 114.6 metres deep in the federal state of California in 1911.

◉ It is warm in Northern Europe because a warm ocean current comes from North America. This is known as the Gulf Stream, and it brings warm air with it.

Driest

The **driest place** on Earth is the **Atacama Desert** in Chile. Between 1964 and 2001, it only had 0.5 mm of rain in 37 years.

Equator

SOUTH AMERICA

Atacama Desert ○

at sea	wind-force	metre/second	on land
hurricane	12	32.7 –	hurricane
severe storm	11	28.5 – 32.6	severe storm
storm	10	24.5 – 28.4	storm
strong gale	9	20.8 – 24.4	strong gale
fresh gale	8	17.2 – 20.7	rough wind
moderate gale	7	13.9 – 17.1	
strong breeze	6	10.8 – 13.8	fresh wind
fresh breeze	5	8.0 – 10.7	
fresh breeze	4	5.5 – 7.9	moderate breeze
moderate breeze	3	3.4 – 5.4	
light breeze	2	1.6 – 3.3	light breeze
almost calm	1	0.3 – 1.5	
calm	0	0.0 – 0.2	calm

The wind can be warm and pleasant in summer and icy cold in winter! If it is blowing a lot, you sometimes want to know how strong it is blowing. The speed is measured in "metres per second". At sea, the thirteen-point **Beaufort** scale is often used. Zero is windless and 12 is a hurricane!

◉ Scientists have discovered that rain-drops don't actually look like drops. They are shaped more like a hamburger bun.

Tornado approaching!

Some different names for winds

➡ **Chinook**
➡ **Cyclone**
➡ **Doctor**
➡ **Föhn wind**
➡ **Mistral**
➡ **Hurricane**
➡ **Sirocco**
➡ **Tornado**
➡ **Typhoon**
➡ **Willy-Willy**

	Very dry	Dry	Rainy	Very rainy
Very cold				
Cold				
Cool				
Warm				
Very warm				

The hottest area is around the **equator**, and it gets colder towards the Poles. Just south or north of the equator, e.g. in the Sahara, it is hot but also drier, as not so much cloud forms there. The tropical areas around the equator receive the most rain.

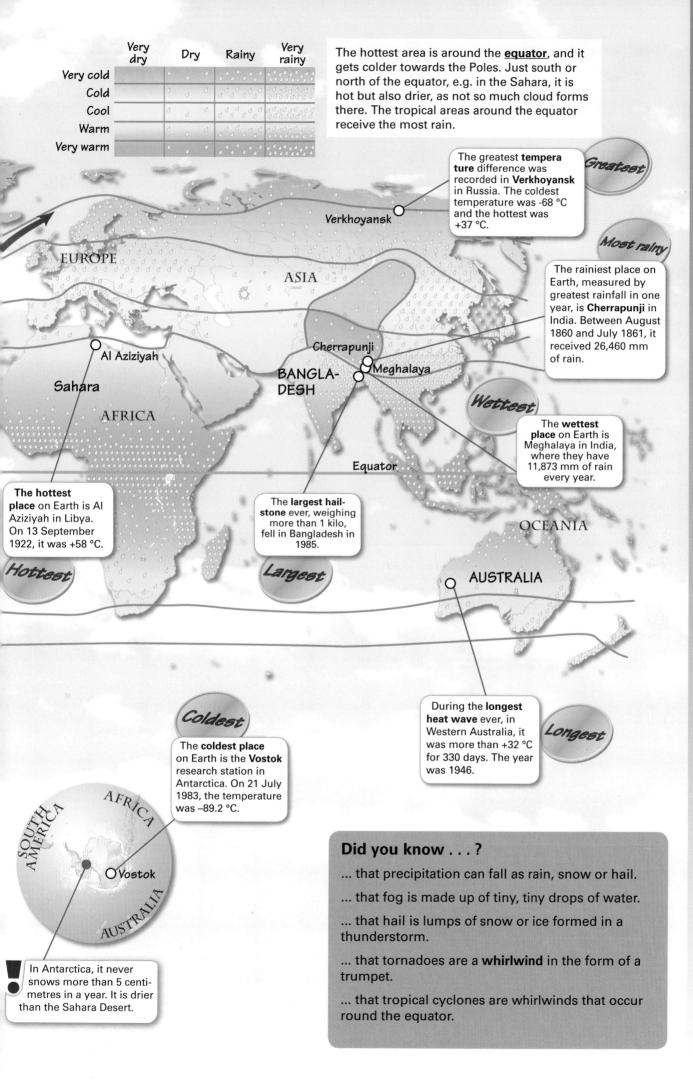

Greatest

The greatest **temperature** difference was recorded in **Verkhoyansk** in Russia. The coldest temperature was -68 °C and the hottest was +37 °C.

Most rainy

The rainiest place on Earth, measured by greatest rainfall in one year, is **Cherrapunji** in India. Between August 1860 and July 1861, it received 26,460 mm of rain.

Wettest

The **wettest place** on Earth is Meghalaya in India, where they have 11,873 mm of rain every year.

Hottest

The hottest place on Earth is Al Aziziyah in Libya. On 13 September 1922, it was +58 °C.

Largest

The **largest hailstone** ever, weighing more than 1 kilo, fell in Bangladesh in 1985.

Longest

During the **longest heat wave** ever, in Western Australia, it was more than +32 °C for 330 days. The year was 1946.

Coldest

The **coldest place** on Earth is the **Vostok** research station in Antarctica. On 21 July 1983, the temperature was –89.2 °C.

In Antarctica, it never snows more than 5 centimetres in a year. It is drier than the Sahara Desert.

EUROPE
ASIA
AFRICA
OCEANIA
AUSTRALIA
SOUTH AMERICA
Verkhoyansk
Al Aziziyah
Sahara
Cherrapunji
Meghalaya
BANGLA-DESH
Equator
Vostok

Did you know . . . ?

... that precipitation can fall as rain, snow or hail.

... that fog is made up of tiny, tiny drops of water.

... that hail is lumps of snow or ice formed in a thunderstorm.

... that tornadoes are a **whirlwind** in the form of a trumpet.

... that tropical cyclones are whirlwinds that occur round the equator.

The Largest OCEANS

1	Pacific Ocean	179 679 000 km²
2	Atlantic Ocean	92 140 000 km²
3	Indian Ocean	74 917 000 km²
4	Arctic Ocean	13 223 800 km²
5	Tasman Sea	6 400 000 km²
6	Coral Sea	4 791 000 km²
7	South China Sea	2 974 600 km²
8	Caribbean Sea	2 515 900 km²
9	Mediterranean Sea	2 505 000 km²
10	Bering Sea	2 261 100 km²

In 1893, Norwegian **polar explorer** Fridtjof Nansen attempted to sail to the **North Pole** in his boat Fram, but he did not manage to cross the Arctic Ocean. **American Robert Peary** got through on foot and was the first to reach the **North Pole**, in 1909.

Arctic Ocean

The **Maldives** island group in the Indian Ocean consists of 1800 islands that are only 2-6 metres above sea level.

Gulf Stream

North Atlantic Ocean

Mediterranean Sea

Dead Sea

Caribbean Sea

The Atlantic Ocean is roughly half as big as the Pacific. The **Gulf Stream** flows from the American **continent** across the North Atlantic up to Northern Europe. This is a warm ocean current that causes Northern Europe's weather to be warmer than it would otherwise be.

Cod, Orca whales, barracuda and eels can all be found in the Atlantic.

The **Caribbean Sea** between the West Indian islands and South America contains one seventh of the world's **coral reefs**.

South Atlantic Ocean

Indian Ocean

The Indian Ocean is the third largest ocean in the world and lies between Africa and Australia. In 1938, an unusual fish was caught in the Indian Ocean. It is called a **coelacanth**. It was thought to be extinct, but specimens have been caught many times since then. The Indian Ocean is also home to many different species of shark, octopus and flying fish.

Did you know . . . ?

... that **tides**, which change the level of the ocean surface and produce **ebb** and **flow**, are the result of the **gravity** of the sun and moon.

... that **tide** differences can be as much as 15 metres.

... that it is now possible to travel by submarine under the ice to the North Pole.

... that the highest temperature recorded in the ocean was 404 degrees **Celsius**, near a discharge of hot water from the ocean floor off the west coast of the USA.

... that the biggest **ocean wave** formed by the wind was 34 metres high.

... that 96.5% of all the water on Earth is salt water.

... that the water of the Dead Sea contains 33% salt, ten times more than in the world's oceans.

The **giant squid** of the Atlantic has the largest eyes of any creature, as large as a basketball.

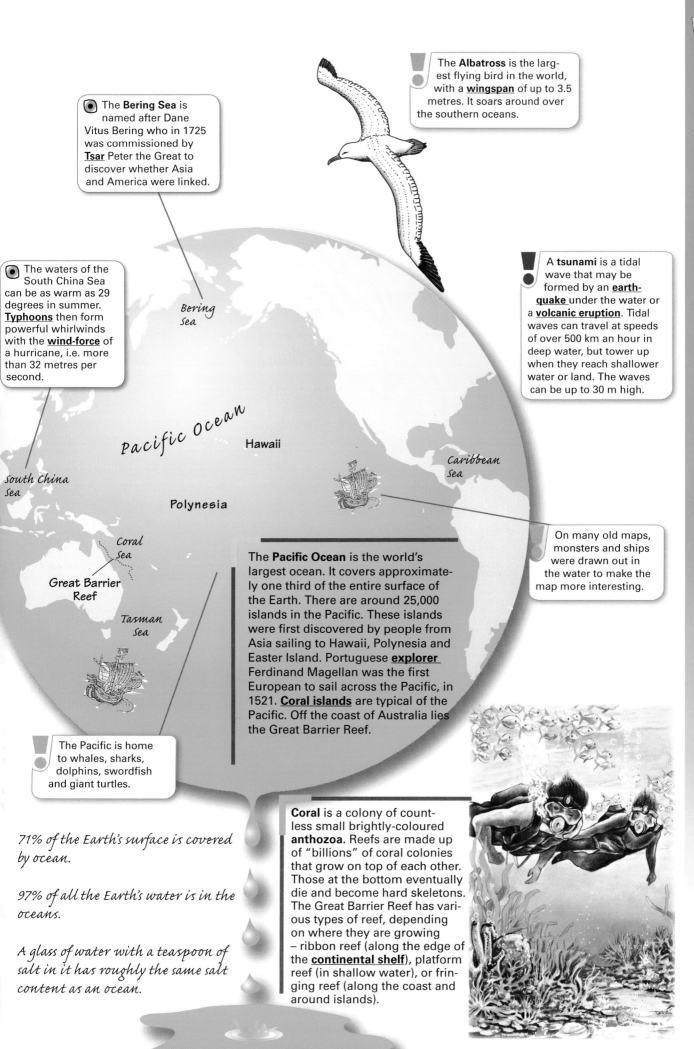

The **Albatross** is the largest flying bird in the world, with a <u>wingspan</u> of up to 3.5 metres. It soars around over the southern oceans.

◉ The **Bering Sea** is named after Dane Vitus Bering who in 1725 was commissioned by <u>Tsar</u> Peter the Great to discover whether Asia and America were linked.

A **tsunami** is a tidal wave that may be formed by an <u>earthquake</u> under the water or a <u>volcanic eruption</u>. Tidal waves can travel at speeds of over 500 km an hour in deep water, but tower up when they reach shallower water or land. The waves can be up to 30 m high.

◉ The waters of the South China Sea can be as warm as 29 degrees in summer. <u>Typhoons</u> then form powerful whirlwinds with the <u>wind-force</u> of a hurricane, i.e. more than 32 metres per second.

Bering Sea

Pacific Ocean

Hawaii

Caribbean Sea

South China Sea

Polynesia

Coral Sea

Great Barrier Reef

Tasman Sea

On many old maps, monsters and ships were drawn out in the water to make the map more interesting.

The **Pacific Ocean** is the world's largest ocean. It covers approximately one third of the entire surface of the Earth. There are around 25,000 islands in the Pacific. These islands were first discovered by people from Asia sailing to Hawaii, Polynesia and Easter Island. Portuguese <u>explorer</u> Ferdinand Magellan was the first European to sail across the Pacific, in 1521. <u>Coral islands</u> are typical of the Pacific. Off the coast of Australia lies the Great Barrier Reef.

The Pacific is home to whales, sharks, dolphins, swordfish and giant turtles.

71% of the Earth's surface is covered by ocean.

97% of all the Earth's water is in the oceans.

A glass of water with a teaspoon of salt in it has roughly the same salt content as an ocean.

Coral is a colony of countless small brightly-coloured **anthozoa**. Reefs are made up of "billions" of coral colonies that grow on top of each other. Those at the bottom eventually die and become hard skeletons. The Great Barrier Reef has various types of reef, depending on where they are growing – ribbon reef (along the edge of the <u>continental shelf</u>), platform reef (in shallow water), or fringing reef (along the coast and around islands).

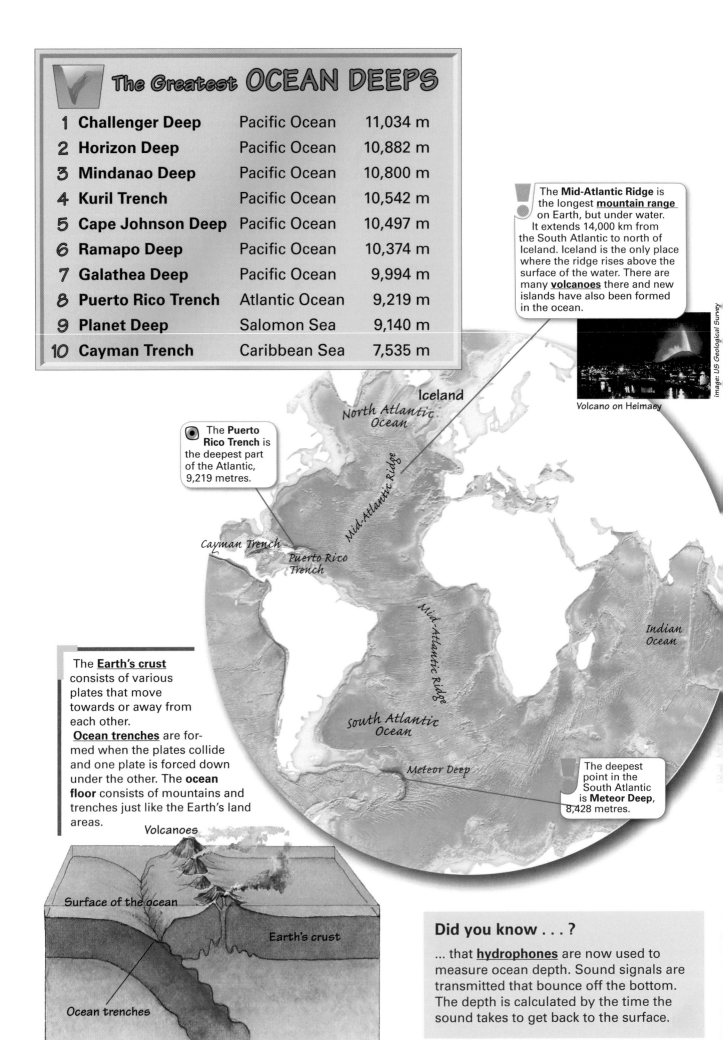

The Greatest OCEAN DEEPS

1	Challenger Deep	Pacific Ocean	11,034 m
2	Horizon Deep	Pacific Ocean	10,882 m
3	Mindanao Deep	Pacific Ocean	10,800 m
4	Kuril Trench	Pacific Ocean	10,542 m
5	Cape Johnson Deep	Pacific Ocean	10,497 m
6	Ramapo Deep	Pacific Ocean	10,374 m
7	Galathea Deep	Pacific Ocean	9,994 m
8	Puerto Rico Trench	Atlantic Ocean	9,219 m
9	Planet Deep	Salomon Sea	9,140 m
10	Cayman Trench	Caribbean Sea	7,535 m

The **Mid-Atlantic Ridge** is the longest **mountain range** on Earth, but under water. It extends 14,000 km from the South Atlantic to north of Iceland. Iceland is the only place where the ridge rises above the surface of the water. There are many **volcanoes** there and new islands have also been formed in the ocean.

Image: US Geological Survey

Volcano on Heimaey

The **Puerto Rico Trench** is the deepest part of the Atlantic, 9,219 metres.

Iceland

North Atlantic Ocean

Mid-Atlantic Ridge

Cayman Trench

Puerto Rico Trench

Mid-Atlantic Ridge

Indian Ocean

South Atlantic Ocean

Meteor Deep

The deepest point in the South Atlantic is **Meteor Deep**, 8,428 metres.

The **Earth's crust** consists of various plates that move towards or away from each other. **Ocean trenches** are formed when the plates collide and one plate is forced down under the other. The **ocean floor** consists of mountains and trenches just like the Earth's land areas.

Volcanoes

Surface of the ocean

Earth's crust

Ocean trenches

Did you know . . . ?

... that **hydrophones** are now used to measure ocean depth. Sound signals are transmitted that bounce off the bottom. The depth is calculated by the time the sound takes to get back to the surface.

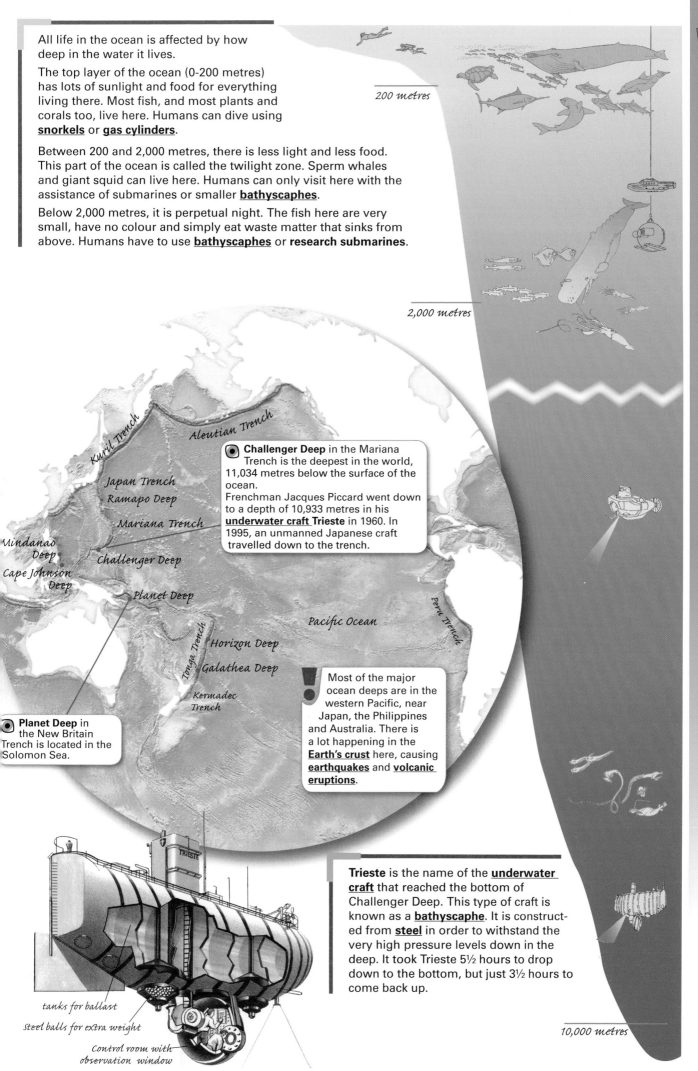

All life in the ocean is affected by how deep in the water it lives.

The top layer of the ocean (0-200 metres) has lots of sunlight and food for everything living there. Most fish, and most plants and corals too, live here. Humans can dive using **snorkels** or **gas cylinders**.

Between 200 and 2,000 metres, there is less light and less food. This part of the ocean is called the twilight zone. Sperm whales and giant squid can live here. Humans can only visit here with the assistance of submarines or smaller **bathyscaphes**.

Below 2,000 metres, it is perpetual night. The fish here are very small, have no colour and simply eat waste matter that sinks from above. Humans have to use **bathyscaphes** or **research submarines**.

200 metres

2,000 metres

Kuril Trench

Aleutian Trench

Japan Trench
Ramapo Deep

Mariana Trench

Mindanao Deep

Cape Johnson Deep

Challenger Deep

Planet Deep

Tonga Trench

Horizon Deep

Galathea Deep

Kermadec Trench

Pacific Ocean

Peru Trench

Challenger Deep in the Mariana Trench is the deepest in the world, 11,034 metres below the surface of the ocean.
Frenchman Jacques Piccard went down to a depth of 10,933 metres in his **underwater craft** Trieste in 1960. In 1995, an unmanned Japanese craft travelled down to the trench.

Planet Deep in the New Britain Trench is located in the Solomon Sea.

Most of the major ocean deeps are in the western Pacific, near Japan, the Philippines and Australia. There is a lot happening in the **Earth's crust** here, causing **earthquakes** and **volcanic eruptions**.

TRIESTE

tanks for ballast

steel balls for extra weight

Control room with observation window

Trieste is the name of the **underwater craft** that reached the bottom of Challenger Deep. This type of craft is known as a **bathyscaphe**. It is constructed from **steel** in order to withstand the very high pressure levels down in the deep. It took Trieste 5½ hours to drop down to the bottom, but just 3½ hours to come back up.

10,000 metres

The Largest LAKES

1	**Caspian Sea**	371,000 km²
2	**Lake Superior**	82,103 km²
3	**Lake Victoria**	69,485 km²
4	**Lake Huron**	59,570 km²
5	**Lake Michigan**	57,866 km²
6	**Lake Tanganyika**	32,893 km²
7	**Lake Baikal**	31,500 km²
8	**Great Bear Lake**	31,328 km²
9	**Lake Malawi**	28,880 km²
10	**Great Slave Lake**	28,568 km²

The **Loch Ness Monster**, also known as Nessie, is a large unknown creature that lives in Loch Ness in Scotland. Many people claim to have seen Nessie and some believe that it is a water-dwelling <u>dinosaur</u> that has survived into our time.

Lake Superior is fed by more than 200 rivers.

Lake Superior

Lake Michigan *Lake Huron*

Great Bear Lake, situated on the Arctic Circle in northern Canada, is only free of ice for 4 months of the year.

The western and northern beaches around **Lake Michigan** consist of soft white sand.

Manitoulin Island, the largest lake island in the world, is in **Lake Huron**.

Great Bear Lake

Great Slave Lake is in the north west of Canada. More animals than people live there.

Great Slave Lake

Lake Athabasca

Lake Winnipeg

Great Salt Lake   **NORTH AMERICA**

Lake Ontario

Lake Erie

The five largest lakes in the eastern USA, **Lake Superior, Lake Michigan, Lake Huron, Lake Erie** and **Lake Ontario**, contain 20% of the world's <u>fresh water</u>.

South America, Africa and Australia do not have that many lakes. Most are in North America and Europe because they were covered by inland ice.

The large Nile Sturgeon fish has been introduced into **Lake Victoria** in Africa, resulting in other fish species now being <u>wiped out</u> in the lake.

SOUTH AMERICA

Lake Titicaca

Lake Titicaca lies between Peru and Bolivia in the Andes mountain range. It is the highest <u>situated</u> lake in the world, 3,810 metres above sea level.

Did you know . . . ?

... that the saltiest lake in the world is the **Dead Sea**. It is so salty that no fish can live there.

... that 20% of the Earth's fresh water is in Lake Baikal.

... that the **Blue Lagoon** in Iceland is a warm man-made lake with a water temperature of 40 °C.

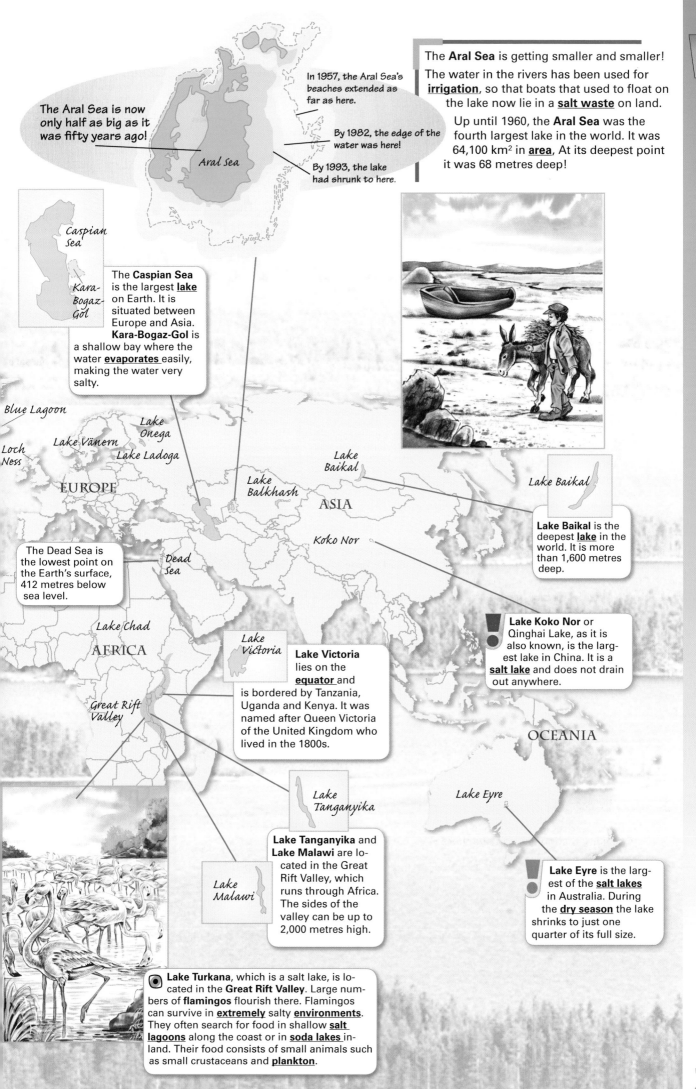

The **Aral Sea** is getting smaller and smaller!

The water in the rivers has been used for **irrigation**, so that boats that used to float on the lake now lie in a **salt waste** on land.

Up until 1960, the **Aral Sea** was the fourth largest lake in the world. It was 64,100 km² in **area**, At its deepest point it was 68 metres deep!

The Aral Sea is now only half as big as it was fifty years ago!

In 1957, the Aral Sea's beaches extended as far as here.

By 1982, the edge of the water was here!

By 1993, the lake had shrunk to here.

Aral Sea

Caspian Sea

Kara-Bogaz-Gol

The **Caspian Sea** is the largest **lake** on Earth. It is situated between Europe and Asia. **Kara-Bogaz-Gol** is a shallow bay where the water **evaporates** easily, making the water very salty.

Blue Lagoon

Loch Ness

Lake Vänern

Lake Onega

Lake Ladoga

EUROPE

Lake Balkhash

Lake Baikal

ASIA

Lake Baikal

Lake Baikal is the deepest **lake** in the world. It is more than 1,600 metres deep.

The Dead Sea is the lowest point on the Earth's surface, 412 metres below sea level.

Dead Sea

Koko Nor

Lake Chad

AFRICA

Lake Victoria

Lake Victoria lies on the **equator** and is bordered by Tanzania, Uganda and Kenya. It was named after Queen Victoria of the United Kingdom who lived in the 1800s.

! **Lake Koko Nor** or Qinghai Lake, as it is also known, is the largest lake in China. It is a **salt lake** and does not drain out anywhere.

Great Rift Valley

OCEANIA

Lake Tanganyika

Lake Eyre

Lake Malawi

Lake Tanganyika and **Lake Malawi** are located in the Great Rift Valley, which runs through Africa. The sides of the valley can be up to 2,000 metres high.

! **Lake Eyre** is the largest of the **salt lakes** in Australia. During the **dry season** the lake shrinks to just one quarter of its full size.

◉ **Lake Turkana**, which is a salt lake, is located in the **Great Rift Valley**. Large numbers of **flamingos** flourish there. Flamingos can survive in **extremely** salty **environments**. They often search for food in shallow **salt lagoons** along the coast or in **soda lakes** inland. Their food consists of small animals such as small crustaceans and **plankton**.

The longest RIVERS

1	**Nile**	6,695 km
2	**Amazon**	6,437 km
3	**Chang Jiang**	6,379 km
4	**Huang He**	5,464 km
5	**Congo**	4,667 km
6	**Lena**	4,400 km
7	**Amur**	4,352 km
8	**Mekong**	4,345 km
9	**Irtysh**	4,248 km
10	**Mackenzie**	4,241 km

Did you know . . . ?

... that an adult needs 3 litres of water per day to survive.

... that the **Ganges** is the **Hindus'** holy river.

... that water can create **ravines**, e.g. **Samaria Gorge** on Crete.

... that humans are made up of 2/3 water.

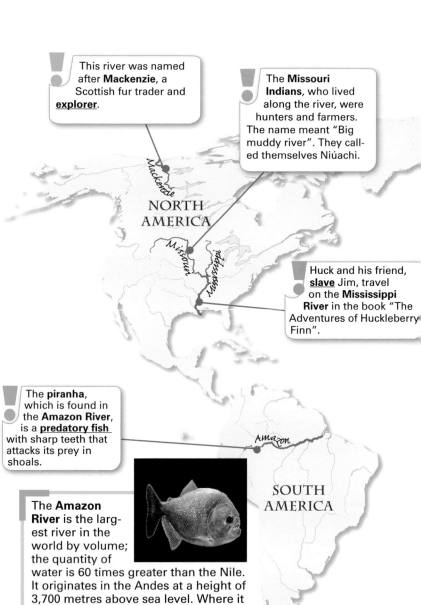

This river was named after **Mackenzie**, a Scottish fur trader and **explorer**.

The **Missouri Indians**, who lived along the river, were hunters and farmers. The name meant "Big muddy river". They called themselves Niúachi.

NORTH AMERICA

Huck and his friend, **slave** Jim, travel on the **Mississippi River** in the book "The Adventures of Huckleberry Finn".

The **piranha**, which is found in the **Amazon River**, is a **predatory fish** with sharp teeth that attacks its prey in shoals.

The **Amazon River** is the largest river in the world by volume; the quantity of water is 60 times greater than the Nile. It originates in the Andes at a height of 3,700 metres above sea level. Where it flows out into the Atlantic it is yellow-coloured from all the **silt** it carries with it. It was discovered by the Spanish back in the 1500s. River dolphins and anaconda live here. There are also many different species of fish, including tetra, electric eels and piranhas.

SOUTH AMERICA

The cycle of water

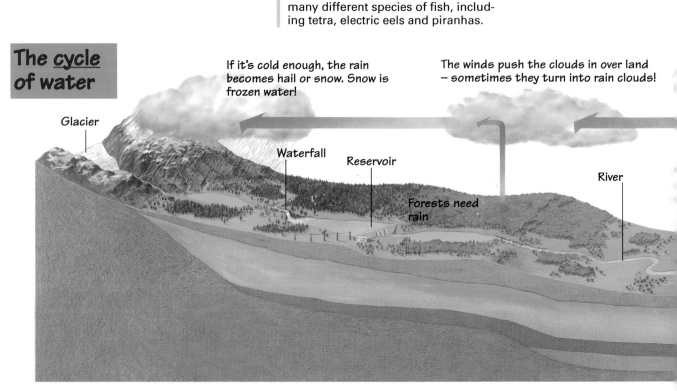

If it's cold enough, the rain becomes hail or snow. Snow is frozen water!

The winds push the clouds in over land – sometimes they turn into rain clouds!

Glacier

Waterfall

Reservoir

Forests need rain

River

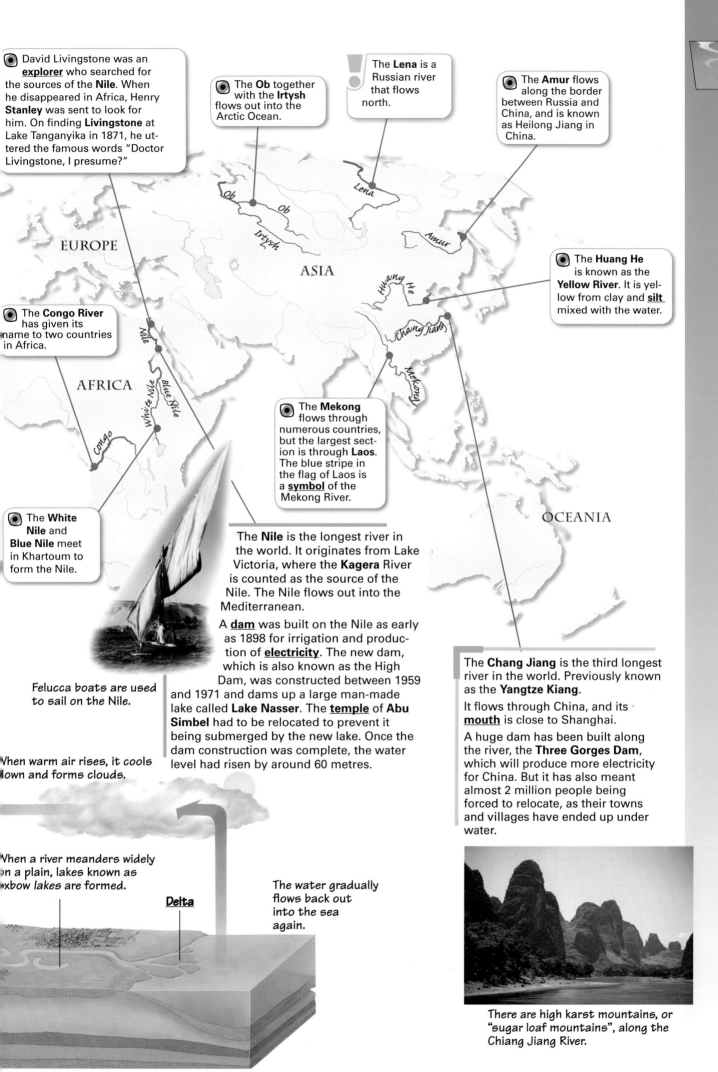

⊙ David Livingstone was an **explorer** who searched for the sources of the **Nile**. When he disappeared in Africa, Henry **Stanley** was sent to look for him. On finding **Livingstone** at Lake Tanganyika in 1871, he uttered the famous words "Doctor Livingstone, I presume?"

⊙ The **Ob** together with the **Irtysh** flows out into the Arctic Ocean.

The **Lena** is a Russian river that flows north.

⊙ The **Amur** flows along the border between Russia and China, and is known as Heilong Jiang in China.

EUROPE

ASIA

⊙ The **Huang He** is known as the **Yellow River**. It is yellow from clay and **silt** mixed with the water.

⊙ The **Congo River** has given its name to two countries in Africa.

AFRICA

⊙ The **Mekong** flows through numerous countries, but the largest section is through **Laos**. The blue stripe in the flag of Laos is a **symbol** of the Mekong River.

OCEANIA

⊙ The **White Nile** and **Blue Nile** meet in Khartoum to form the Nile.

The **Nile** is the longest river in the world. It originates from Lake Victoria, where the **Kagera** River is counted as the source of the Nile. The Nile flows out into the Mediterranean.

A **dam** was built on the Nile as early as 1898 for irrigation and production of **electricity**. The new dam, which is also known as the High Dam, was constructed between 1959 and 1971 and dams up a large man-made lake called **Lake Nasser**. The **temple** of **Abu Simbel** had to be relocated to prevent it being submerged by the new lake. Once the dam construction was complete, the water level had risen by around 60 metres.

Felucca boats are used to sail on the Nile.

When warm air rises, it cools down and forms clouds.

When a river meanders widely on a plain, lakes known as oxbow lakes are formed.

Delta

The water gradually flows back out into the sea again.

The **Chang Jiang** is the third longest river in the world. Previously known as the **Yangtze Kiang**.

It flows through China, and its **mouth** is close to Shanghai.

A huge dam has been built along the river, the **Three Gorges Dam**, which will produce more electricity for China. But it has also meant almost 2 million people being forced to relocate, as their towns and villages have ended up under water.

There are high karst mountains, or "sugar loaf mountains", along the Chiang Jiang River.

The Highest WATERFALLS

1	Angel Falls	Venezuela	979 m
2	Tugela Falls	South Africa	947 m
3	Kjelfossen	Norway	840 m
4	Mtarazi Falls	Zimbabwe	762 m
5	Yosemite Falls	USA	739 m
6	Southern Mardalsfoss	Norway	705 m
7	Mongefossen	Norway	700 m
8	Eastern Mardalsfoss	Norway	655 m
9	Opo	Norway	650 m
10	Vedalsfossen	Norway	650 m

Niagara Falls lies on the border between the USA and Canada

Angel Falls, which is located in Venezuela, is 979 metres high. The falls are 16 times higher than Niagara Falls, and were discovered by an **American**, **Jimmy Angel,** in 1933 while searching for gold in Guyana. In 1937, he returned and landed his plane at the top of the falls. The plane got stuck and it took the occupants 11 days to make their way out on foot. The plane remained there for 33 years before being lifted out by a helicopter.

NORTH AMERICA

Yosemite Falls

Niagara Falls

Yosemite Falls are situated in the Yosemite **national park**, which is on **UNESCO**'s list of **world heritage** sites, sites to be protected and preserved.

Angel Falls

SOUTH AMERICA

Iguaçu Falls

Kjelfossen (Kjell Falls) in Norway flows out into Næroyfjord in Sognefjord.

Southern Mardalsfoss

Eastern Mardalsfoss

Mongefossen

Kjelfossen

Vedalsfossen

Opo

NORWAY

EUROPE

ASIA

AFRICA

There are many waterfalls in the Norwegian landscape. **Kjelfossen, Southern Mardalsfoss, Eastern Mardalsfoss, Mongefossen, Opo** and **Vedalsfossen** are all in Norway and are among the 10 highest waterfalls in the world, measured by free **drop**.

Did you know . . . ?

... that a seven-year-old boy who was swept over Niagara Falls following a boat accident survived the fall thanks to the fact that he was wearing a life jacket.

... that Iguaçu Falls has 9 times more water than Niagara Falls.

Mtarazi Falls is located in eastern Zimbabwe in Africa. The area is a **national park**, to protect the falls.

Victoria Falls

Mtarazi Falls

Tugela Falls

OCEANIA

Tugela Falls is South Africa's highest waterfall. It is located in the **Drakensberg** in South Africa.

Other famous waterfalls

Victoria Falls is located on the Zambezi River on the border between Zimbabwe and Zambia. In **Bantu**, the falls are known as Mosi-oa-tunya, which means "The smoke that thunders". **Missionary** David Livingstone was the first European to see the falls, in 1855.

Niagara Falls on the border between the USA and Canada is probably the most famous waterfall in the world. Many people visit there nowadays to celebrate birthdays and weddings. A number of **reckless** people have gone over the falls in various types of barrel; not all of them survived this dangerous trip.

Iguaçu Falls on the border between Brazil and Argentina is almost 3 kilometres wide. The water is brown-coloured, as it contains a lot of **silt**.

ANIMALS OF THE WORLD

Longest The tallest **mammal** is the **giraffe**. A male can be between 3.4 and 4.5 metres tall. Even though its neck is so long, it only has seven cervical vertebrae, just like humans. The giraffe has a black tongue, which can be up to 45 cm long. It uses this to pull leaves off trees.

The giraffe lives on Africa's **savannahs**, south of the Sahara.

Oldest The oldest **mammal** is the **Indian elephant**, which can be up to 70, possibly even 80, years old. It is smaller than the African elephant. The Indian elephant has five nails on its forefeet and four on its hind feet.

It lives in India and Southeast Asia.

Smallest The smallest bird in the world is a **colibri** (humming bird). The male is 56 mm long and weighs just 1.6 grams. It hovers in the air using its humming wings. It lives in Cuba.

Slowest The slowest **mammal** is the **three-toed sloth**. It moves at a speed of 2 metres a minute. The sloth hangs upside down and eats leaves. Once a week it has to descend to the ground and find a suitable toilet spot. It lives in Central and South America.

! A reindeer in North America is also known as a **caribou**, which is an Indian name for reindeer.

NORTH AMERICA

ATLANTIC OCEAN

Cuba

! The **toucan** is a bird with a brightly-coloured bill that is just as long as its body.

PACIFIC OCEAN

CENTRAL AMERICA

! The **Spider monkey** of South America has long arms and legs. It also uses its tail for holding on to branches.

SOUTH AMERICA

The world's largest bird is the **ostrich**, a flightless bird. A male ostrich can be up to 2.75 metres tall and weigh over 150 kilos. An ostrich egg can bear the weight of a human up to 115 kilos without breaking. An ostrich egg is equivalent to 18 hen's eggs and takes 40 minutes to boil.

Largest

The largest **mammal** is the **blue whale**. It can be up to 30 metres long and weigh 150 tons. A full-grown blue whale eats 4.5 tons of plankton every day. A newborn blue whale calf drinks 190 litres of milk per day and puts on weight at a rate of 3.5 kilos per hour. Blue whales can be found in all the world's oceans.

Largest

The **sea wasp** is a **jellyfish** containing sufficient venom to kill 60 humans. If you come into contact with one of these, you can die within 30 seconds. It lives in the waters north of Australia.

Most poisonous

Fastest

The fastest fish in the world is the **sailfish**. It can reach speeds of up to 120 km/h. It is also the strongest and most spirited fighter of all game fish. Unlike the **swordfish** and **spearfish**, it is sociable. Shoals of 40 specimens have sometimes been sighted.

Did you know . . . ?

... that the longest horn on a **rhinoceros** was measured at 158 cm.

... that both **pumas** and **leopards** can leap 5 metres up into a tree.

... that the **wandering albatross** has the largest wingspan of any bird, up to 3.7 metres.

... that the heaviest insect in the world is the **Goliath beetle**, which can weigh up to 100 grams.

The **beaver** is the largest <u>rodent</u> in Europe, and the second largest in the world. Only the **capybara** in South America is larger.

The fastest bird in the world is the **peregrine falcon**.

Longest

The longest snake ever measured was a **reticulated python**, which was 10 metres long when it was shot on Sulawesi in 1912.

EUROPE

ASIA

Sahara
AFRICA

Pumbaa in the Disney film 'The Lion King' is a **warthog** who lives in Africa.

Sulawesi

PACIFIC OCEAN

INDIAN OCEAN

OCEANIA

New Zealand has no dangerous or poisonous animals.

Largest

The **African elephant** is the largest land <u>mammal</u>. A male can be up to 3.7 metres tall and weigh 7 tons. An elephant calf weighs 1 ton by the age of 6. The calf may drink its mother's milk for up to ten years. It has larger ears than the Indian **elephant**. It has five nails on its forefeet, but only 3 on its hind feet. It lives in Africa, south of the Sahara.

Fastest

The fastest <u>mammal</u> in the world is the **cheetah**. It can reach a speed of up to 100 km per hour. It can only keep this up for a minute, and it then has to rest. It can be found in eastern and southern Africa. The **king cheetah's** spots are larger, and sometimes almost stripes. Cheetah cubs stay with their mother until they are around 1.5 years old.

Oldest

One specimen of the **Madagascan radiated tortoise** lived to the age of 188. It was presented to the royal family of <u>Tonga</u> by Captain Cook who sailed the Pacific in the 1770s. The tortoise lived right up to 1965.

The Largest COUNTRIES

1	Russia	17,075,200 km²
2	Canada	9,976,140 km²
3	USA	9,629,091 km²
4	China	9,596,960 km²
5	Brazil	8,511,965 km²
6	Australia	7,617,930 km²
7	India	3,287,590 km²
8	Argentina	2,766,890 km²
9	Kazakhstan	2,717,300 km²
10	Sudan	2,505,810 km²

Canada's land area is two-fifths of the whole of North America, and almost half of Canada is covered by forest.

Europeans came to Canada at the end of the 1400s, and it has been both an English and French **colony**. Consequently, both French and English are spoken in different parts of the country.

The northernmost parts of the country are virtually **uninhabited**.

The **USA's** smallest state by area is **Rhode Island**, the largest is Alaska.

Canada's parliament buildings in Ottawa

Alaska

CANADA

Ottawa

USA

Rhode Island

Washington DC

The White House in Washington

Brasília Cathedral

USA stands for the **United States of America**.

The USA is now made up of 50 **states**. The first 13 states formed a **union** in 1776; **Alaska** and **Hawaii** did not become states until 1959.

The original population of America was **Indians** and **Inuit**. Indians are called that because **Columbus**, who discovered America in 1492, thought that he had come to India.

BRAZIL

Brasília

The **Tango** in **Argentina** is thought to originate from the black **slaves'** dancing from the early 1800s.

Argentina's name comes from the Spanish word for silver, argento, and it is probably named after the silver that explorers bartered from the **aborigines**.

Buenos Aires

ARGENTINA

Brazil's largest cities are **Sao Paolo** and **Rio de Janeiro**, but its **capital** is Brasília. It was specially designed and built to become the capital, which it did on 21 April 1960.

A flag is such a strong symbol of a country that it is often sufficient to show the flag instead of the country's name. At large sporting events it is common to use flags to indicate the competitors' countries. The clothing of the competitors is also often the same colour as their country's flag.

Brazil

Australia

India

Argentina

Kazakhstan

Sudan

China

Did you know . . . ?

... that the **Vatican State** is the world's smallest country, in terms of both area and number of inhabitants.

... that **Mongolia** is the most sparsely-populated country in the world, with 1.6 inhabitants per km².

... that **Monaco** is the most **densely-populated** country in the world, with 16,307 inhabitants per km².

... that there are 194 **independent** states in the world.

Kazakhstan is one of the countries that became a new state in 1991 following the __dissolution__ of the Soviet Union. In 1997, the __capital__ was moved from **Alma-Ata** to **Astana**.

Russia is the largest country in the world by area, 17,075,200 km².

The **Trans-Siberian Railway** from Moscow to Vladivostok is 9,300 kilometres long and was completed back in 1915. The entire journey takes 7.5 __days__.

Russia is so huge that it is not the same time across the whole country. While they are eating breakfast in Moscow, people on the Kamchatka Peninsula are already eating dinner.

Saint Basil's Cathedral in Moscow

Russia's neighbours are Norway, Finland, Estonia, Latvia, Lithuania, Poland, Belarus, Ukraine, Georgia, Azerbaijan, Kazakhstan, North Korea, Mongolia and China.

RUSSIA

• Moscow

Astana
KAZAKSTAN

Kamchatka Peninsula

Russia and **China** are the two countries that share a border with the largest number of countries, 14 in total.

Beijing •
CHINA

Kazakhstan is partly in Europe and partly in Asia.

• Delhi
INDIA

The largest structure in the world, the Great Wall of China, can be found in **China**. It is 6,400 kilometres long, 8 metres high and has 24,000 watchtowers.

Khartoum
•
SUDAN

India's __Hindus__ consider cows to be holy, and they may not be killed.

Australia has the world's largest __coral reef__, the Great Barrier Reef, where dangerous great white sharks can be found.

AUSTRALIA

Sudan is the largest country in Africa and is __dominated__ by the huge River Nile flowing through it.

Canberra •

Australia forms part of the continent of Oceania and is most famous for the __boomerang__, which is a throwing stick that returns to the thrower if thrown correctly.

LIECHTENSTEIN
MONACO
ANDORRA   SAN MARINO
THE VATICAN STATE

The smallest countries in the world

- The Vatican State
- Monaco
  Nauru
  Tuvalu
  Bermuda
- San Marino
- Liechtenstein
  The Marshall Islands
  Saint Kitts and Nevis
  The Maldives

Malta
Grenada
Saint Vincent and
  the Grenadines
Barbados
Antigua and Barbuda
The Seychelles
- Andorra

• 5 of the smallest countries in the world are in Europe!

The Largest CITIES

1	**Tokyo**	Japan
2	**New York**	USA
3	**Mexico city**	Mexico
4	**Seoul**	S. Korea
5	**Sao Paulo**	Brasil
6	**Mumbai (Bombay)**	India
7	**Osaka**	Japan
8	**Delhi**	India
9	**Los Angeles**	USA
10	**Jakarta**	Indonesia

New York's most famous statue is the **Statue of Liberty**, which was given to the American people by France. It is 46 metres high and stands on a pedestal that is 47 metres high. It was opened in 1886.
New York, like many other large cities, has various **city districts** that are populated by different ethnic groups.
Chinatown is one example; many Chinese live there.

Los Angeles is often shortened to L.A. Its **city districts** include **Hollywood**, which is known for its film industry, and **Beverly Hills**, where many film and TV stars live. Outside the Los Angeles area you will also find the first Disneyland, which was opened in 1955.

At the Olympic Games in **Mexico City** in 1968, **Bob Beamon** set his famous long jump record of 8.90 metres. This record stood for 23 years, until Mike Powell jumped 8.95 metres in 1991.

Mexico City is situated on a **mountain plateau** 2,300 metres above sea level. The city is sinking at a rate of about 15 cm/year. It is built on an underground lake.

Sao Paulo is a large **industrial city** in Brazil. It is also home to the Santos football club, where the famous footballer Pelé played.

NORTH AMERICA

New York
21.199.900 habitants

Los Angeles
16.373.600 habitants

Mexico
19.125.000 habitants

SOUTH AMERICA

Sao Paulo
17. 833.700 habitants

Did you know . . . ?

... that a **capital city** is the city where the government and parliament of a country are located.

... that the world's first city was **Jericho**, which is now on the West Bank.

... that the city of **Pompeii** in Italy was buried by a **volcanic eruption** in 79 AD.

In 1606, some Dutch **seafarers** discovered an island that the Indians called Manahatta. They traded some goods for the island and called it New Amsterdam. It was later captured by the British, who renamed it **New York**.

New York is now made up of five **city districts**: Manhattan, the Bronx, Brooklyn, Queens and Richmond.

Most streets on the island of **Manhattan** run either from north to south and are called **avenues,** or from west to east and are called streets. They are all numbered, making it easy to find your way around New York.

The pictures show a type of hotel that can be found in **Tokyo**.

They are for people who aren't able to get home between two full **working days**. They can stay overnight in a sleeping cubicle like this.

⊙ **Moscow** has been the **capital city** of the Soviet Republic since 1918 and became the **capital** of Russia in 1991. The **Kremlin**, which in Russian means fortress, is a complex in the heart of Moscow surrounded by walls. These walls now enclose the **tsar's** large **palace** and numerous museums.

⊙ **Kolkata**, which was also known as **Calcutta**, is the **capital** of West Bengal in India. The city is known for its large **slum areas** and the fact that many people live on the streets.

⊙ **Tokyo's** underground railway was opened in 1925 and is now the largest in the world reckoned by number of **passengers**. There are special "platform pushers" who help to fill the carriages during **rush hour**.

Moscou
14.188.600 habitants

EUROPE

ASIA

Le Cairo
13.593.500 habitants

Osaka
17.422.000 habitants

Tokyo
35.374.700 habitants

Mumbai
17.655.400 habitants

Kolkata
13.556.700 habitants

AFRICA

⊙ **Osaka** was already an important port in Japan back in the 700s. Osaka has now merged with a number of other towns, forming a metropolitan area known as Hanshin.

⊙ **Cairo** has been the **capital city** of Egypt since its independence in 1922.
Just outside Cairo, at Giza, are the pyramids, which are royal **tombs**.

⊙ **Mumbai** was formerly known as **Bombay** and was originally built on several small islands that have now been merged. Mumbai is one of the world's most densely-populated cities.

OCEANIA

❗ **Mumbai** is the entertainment capital of India and the name **Bollywood** is used for the **film industry** there. The films are often an exotic mix of song, dance, love and suspense. They are often fairly long.

Tokyo, which means "Eastern capital" was called **Edo** up until 1868. Tokyo is on the east coast of the largest of the Japanese islands, Honshu. Most of Tokyo was destroyed in a major **earthquake** in 1923.

The Olympic Games were held in Tokyo in 1964.

The POPULATION of the world

1	China	1,316 million	people
2	India	1,103 million	"
3	USA	298 million	"
4	Indonesia	235 million	"
5	Brazil	186 million	"
6	Pakistan	158 million	"
7	Russia	143 million	"
8	Bangladesh	142 million	"
9	Nigeria	134 million	"
10	Japan	128 million	"

These are the countries with the fewest inhabitants!

Vatican City	900	people
Tuvalu	11,000	"
Nauru	12,000	"
San Marino	28,000	"
Monaco	32,000	"
Liechtenstein	33,000	"
Saint Kitts and Nevis	38,000	"
The Marshall Islands	56,000	"
Bermuda	64,000	"
Antigua and Barbuda	68,000	"

At the end of 2006 there were **6,555,336 million** people in the world. More than six and a half billion. Nearly 2 billion of these are children. Africa is the <u>continent</u> with the most children.

The **population** of the world has increased from 1 billion in 1800 to 6.5 billion today. By 2050 there will be over 9 billion people.

The population of the **USA** is made up of many different peoples. Most are <u>descendants</u> of people who moved to the USA from other parts of the world. Many <u>slaves</u> were brought from Africa in the 1600s and 1700s. Today, the number of Spanish-speaking <u>inhabitants</u> is increasing.

India's 1 billion people are divided into different <u>castes</u>. You are born into a caste. The caste you belong to determines what occupation you will have and who you can marry. Attempts are now being made to change these customs, but they are still hugely significant in India.

NORTH AMERICA

USA

BERMUDA

ANTIGUA and BARBUDA

SAINT KITTS and NEVIS

! The USA's original **population**, Native Americans, now only make up 1 % of the entire population.

BRAZIL

SOUTH AMERICA

● **Brazil** has a mixed population made up of <u>descendants</u> of African <u>slaves</u>, Portuguese <u>seafarers</u> and the indigenous Indians.

China is the most densely-populated country in the world. Most of the population live in eastern China. There are more than 2,000 people per km² along the Chang Jiang river. In order to limit the increase in population, the <u>government</u> of China decided in the 1980s that each family would only be allowed to have one child.

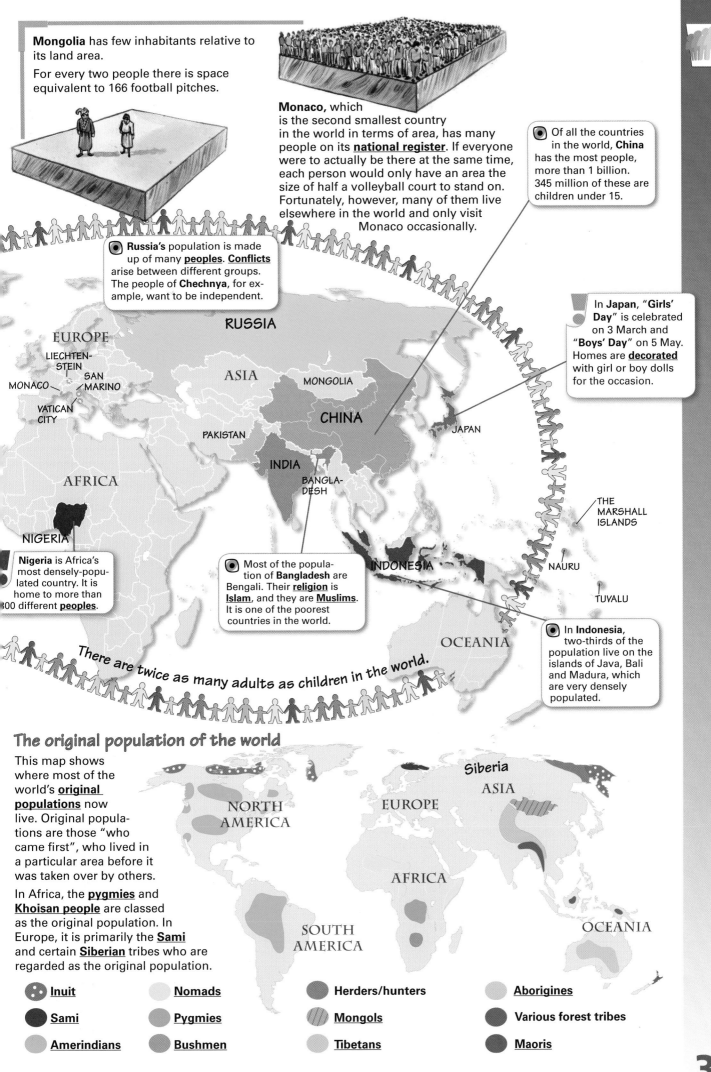

Mongolia has few inhabitants relative to its land area.

For every two people there is space equivalent to 166 football pitches.

Monaco, which is the second smallest country in the world in terms of area, has many people on its **national register**. If everyone were to actually be there at the same time, each person would only have an area the size of half a volleyball court to stand on. Fortunately, however, many of them live elsewhere in the world and only visit Monaco occasionally.

Of all the countries in the world, **China** has the most people, more than 1 billion. 345 million of these are children under 15.

Russia's population is made up of many **peoples**. **Conflicts** arise between different groups. The people of **Chechnya**, for example, want to be independent.

In **Japan**, "Girls' Day" is celebrated on 3 March and "Boys' Day" on 5 May. Homes are **decorated** with girl or boy dolls for the occasion.

RUSSIA

EUROPE

LIECHTEN-STEIN
SAN MARINO
MONACO
VATICAN CITY

ASIA

MONGOLIA

CHINA

PAKISTAN

JAPAN

INDIA

BANGLA-DESH

AFRICA

NIGERIA

THE MARSHALL ISLANDS

Nigeria is Africa's most densely-populated country. It is home to more than 300 different **peoples**.

Most of the population of **Bangladesh** are Bengali. Their **religion** is **Islam**, and they are **Muslims**. It is one of the poorest countries in the world.

INDONESIA

NAURU

TUVALU

OCEANIA

In **Indonesia**, two-thirds of the population live on the islands of Java, Bali and Madura, which are very densely populated.

There are twice as many adults as children in the world.

The original population of the world

This map shows where most of the world's **original populations** now live. Original populations are those "who came first", who lived in a particular area before it was taken over by others.

In Africa, the **pygmies** and **Khoisan people** are classed as the original population. In Europe, it is primarily the **Sami** and certain **Siberian** tribes who are regarded as the original population.

NORTH AMERICA

SOUTH AMERICA

EUROPE

AFRICA

ASIA

Siberia

OCEANIA

Inuit	Nomads	Herders/hunters	Aborigines
Sami	Pygmies	Mongols	Various forest tribes
Amerindians	Bushmen	Tibetans	Maoris

The Most Widely-Spoken LANGUAGES

#			
1	1,000 mill.	speak	**Chinese**
2	512 mill.	"	**English**
3	498 mill.	"	**Hindi**
4	391 mill.	"	**Spanish**
5	280 mill.	"	**Russian**
6	245 mill.	"	**Arabic**
7	211 mill.	"	**Bengali**
8	192 mill.	"	**Portuguese**
9	160 mill.	"	**Indonesian**
10	125 mill.	"	**Japanese**

A B C D E F G H I J

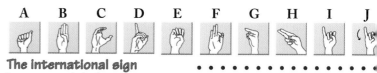

The international sign language alphabet

SIGN LANGUAGE

Being **deaf** means that you cannot hear. The deaf learn to "speak" using their hands and use signs to form words and whole sentences.

The letters above are often used for spelling a word or name.

The map shows where different languages are spoken

Creole languages originated on the **sugar cane plantations** in the southern USA. **Plantation owners** from other countries, e.g. France, mixed their own language with what was already spoken there.

Did you know . . . ?

... that 417 languages are on the list of **endangered** languages throughout the world.

... that 7 of the endangered languages are in Europe.

Chinese

English

Hindi

Spanish

Russian

Arabic

Bengali

Portuguese

Indonesian

Japanese

Many people also speak some of these languages
- **German**
- **Korean**
- **French**

Runic characters

The **Rök Runestone** is located in Sweden. The **runes** were carved at the beginning of the 800s, and the stone, which is two and a half metres tall, is covered with runes on every side. The runes tell, in the language of the time, of people who once lived at the location where the stone was raised. The text can sometimes be difficult to decipher, and the rune inscriber may have left out letters or perhaps made spelling mistakes!

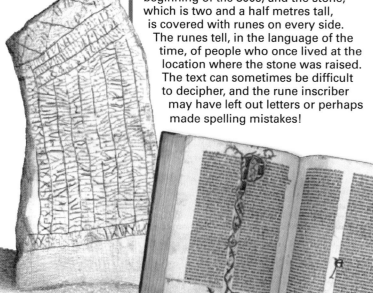

The first printed book in Europe

Monks in Europe began producing books in the 1200s. The few **universities** in existence at that time wanted books for their students. The books were written by hand and took a long time to make.

Johann Gutenberg from Germany is said to be the person who invented the art of printing books. He produced the very first printed book in Europe. This was a bible and was printed some time between 1450 and 1455.

Many different languages are spoken in the light brown countries

There are several thousand languages in the world, depending on how you count.

SMILEYS are also a kind of sign language, which you can use in e-mails to indicate an emotion.

:-)	happy
l-)	laughter
:-o	what?
:-(	sad
: `(	crying
8-)	sunglasses
:-[	vampire
l l	sleeping
@:-)	wearing a turban
:-X	saying nothing
*:o)	clown

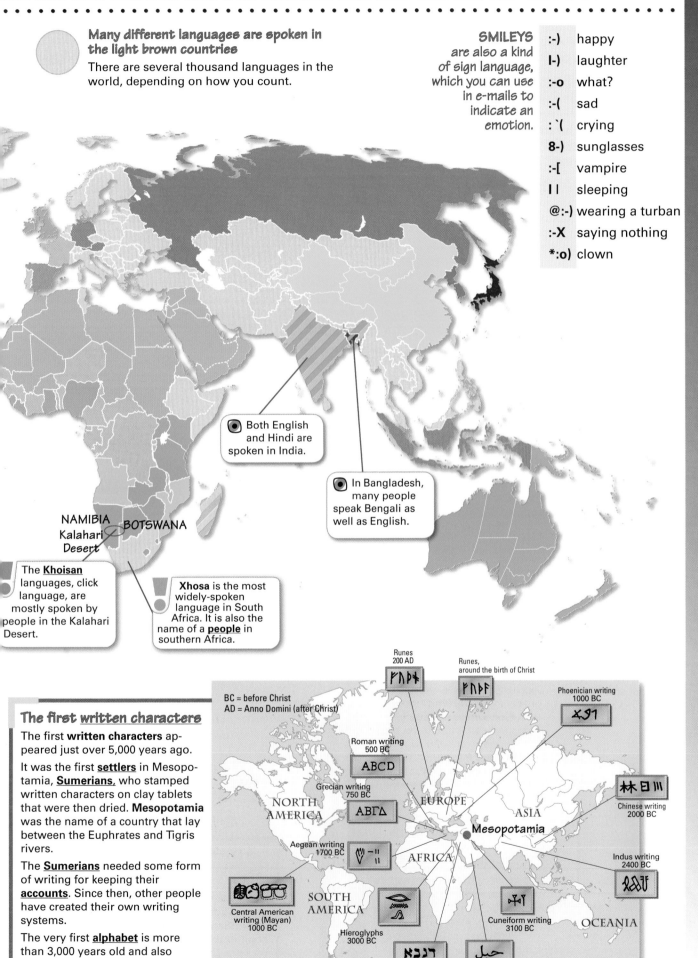

Both English and Hindi are spoken in India.

In Bangladesh, many people speak Bengali as well as English.

NAMIBIA
Kalahari Desert
BOTSWANA

The **Khoisan** languages, click language, are mostly spoken by people in the Kalahari Desert.

Xhosa is the most widely-spoken language in South Africa. It is also the name of a **people** in southern Africa.

The first written characters

The first **written characters** appeared just over 5,000 years ago.

It was the first **settlers** in Mesopotamia, **Sumerians**, who stamped written characters on clay tablets that were then dried. **Mesopotamia** was the name of a country that lay between the Euphrates and Tigris rivers.

The **Sumerians** needed some form of writing for keeping their **accounts**. Since then, other people have created their own writing systems.

The very first **alphabet** is more than 3,000 years old and also emerged in the **Middle East**.

BC = before Christ
AD = Anno Domini (after Christ)

Runes 200 AD

Runes, around the birth of Christ

Phoenician writing 1000 BC

Roman writing 500 BC
ABCD

Grecian writing 750 BC
ABΓΔ

NORTH AMERICA

EUROPE

ASIA

Chinese writing 2000 BC

Mesopotamia

Aegean writing 1700 BC

AFRICA

Indus writing 2400 BC

Central American writing (Mayan) 1000 BC

SOUTH AMERICA

Cuneiform writing 3100 BC

OCEANIA

Hieroglyphs 3000 BC

Hebrew writing, around the birth of Christ

Arabic writing 600 AD

41

OLYMPIADS

The **Olympic Games** of ancient Greece were held at Mount Olympia in southern Greece.

The first Games were held in 776 B.C. The Games were held once every Olympiad; an **Olympiad** is equivalent to four years. The Olympic flame was carried out, and war was banned during the Games.

Only "free Greeks" were allowed to take part at that time. The participants were mostly athletes who lived close to Olympus.

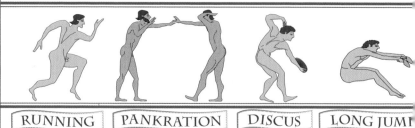

| RUNNING | PANKRATION | DISCUS | LONG JUMP |

The ancient Olympic Games were athletic contests held over five days. At the start, only one sport, running, was included, and it lasted one day. The number of sports was gradually increased to nine.

● SUMMER OLYMPIAD
◉ WINTER OLYMPIAD

Calgary 1988

Montreal 1976

Salt Lake City 2002

Saint-Louis 1904

Lake Placid 1932 and 1980

Squaw Valley 1960

Los Angeles 1932 and 1984

Atlanta 1996

Mexico City 1968

Future Olympic Games:

Beijing, China 2008

Vancouver, Canada 2010

London, United Kingdom 2012

The Olympic Games

The founder of the modern Olympic Games was Frenchman **Pierre de Coubertin**. The first modern Games took place in Athens in 1896.

The sports included in those Games were wrestling, cycling, athletics, fencing, gymnastics, swimming, shooting, tennis and weightlifting. The Greeks wanted the Games to always be held in Athens, but the International Olympic Committee did not agree. In 1906, the Greeks held their own Games between the ordinary Games, but this did not continue.

In 1900, women took part for the first time.

The Olympic Winter Games have been held since 1924. Initially these were held in the same year as the Summer Games. From 1994, the Winter Games were moved to 2 years after each Summer Games.

Most sports are included by <u>tradition</u>, but new sports are sometimes added.

The Olympic oath

At the opening ceremony of each Olympic Games, one of the participants takes the Olympic oath: "In the name of all the competitor I promise that we shall take part in these Olympic Games, respecting and abiding by the rules whic govern them, committing ourselv to a sport without doping and without drugs, in the true spirit of sportsmanship, for the glory of sport and the honour of our team

The Olympic flag

was first used at the Games in 1920, although it first appeared back in 1914.

The colours of the rings are **symbols** of the different **continents**: Europe, Africa, Asia, America, and Oceania.

The Olympic flame

Since 1936, a burning <u>torch</u> has been carried in at the opening ceremony of the Games. The Olympic flame is then lit, and burns throughout the duration of the Games. The torch <u>relay</u> involves countless different runners and sets off from Olympia in Greece. The flame is a <u>symbol</u> of peace.

JAVELIN   WRESTLING   BOXING   RACING WITH HORSE AND CARRIAGE

The pictures show the various sports.

In races involving horses and carriages, it was the horse owner who got the credit if the horse won, and not the driver. This was one way for women to win at an Olympiad, as they could be the **breeder** of a winning horse! **Pankration** is a sport that would probably not be allowed in modern Olympiads. It mostly consisted of kicking and punching!

Amsterdam 1928

Lillehammer 1994

Stockholm 1912

Antwerp 1920

Oslo 1952

Helsinki 1952

Berlin 1936

London 1908 and 1948

Moscow 1980

Munich 1972

Garmisch-Partenkirchen 1936

Paris 1900 and 1924

Seoul 1988

Sapporo 1972

Innsbruck 1964 and 1976

Barcelona 1992

Nagano 1998

Cortina 1956

Grenoble 1968

Sarajevo 1984

Rome 1960

Albertville 1992

Athens 1896 and 2004

Tokyo 1964

Chamonix 1924

St. Moritz 1928 and 1948

Turin 2006

ATHENS 2004

◉ Posters for the Summer Olympiads in Athens in 1896 and 2004.

IOC/Olympic Museum Collections

Sydney 2000

Melbourne 1956

Some winners

● **Paavo Nurmi** from Finland took five Golds in athletics in Paris in 1924.

● In Rome in 1960, **Boris Shakhlin** from the Soviet Union won seven gymnastics medals.

● American **Bob Beamon** won the long jump with an unbelievable 8.90 m in Mexico in 1968.

● **Mark Spitz** from the USA won seven swimming Golds in Munich in 1972.

● In 1984, **Carl Lewis** from the USA won four athletics Golds in Los Angeles.

❗ Each new Olympic Games is larger than the previous one, with more sports and more participants. The proportion of women has increased from zero to almost 50%. Here is a table of some of the Games over the years.

Location (summer/winter)	sports	participating countries	participants men	women
1896 Athens (s)	43	14	241	0
1924 Paris (s)	126	44	2,954	135
1924 Chamonix (w)	16	16	247	11
1928 Amsterdam (s)	109	46	2,600	227
1960 Rome (s)	150	83	4,727	611
1972 Munich (s)	195	121	5,263	1,566
1992 Albertville (w)	57	64	1,313	488
1992 Barcelona (s)	257	169	6,652	2,704
2004 Athens (s)	301	202	8,296	4,329

Ancient WONDERS

1 The **Great Pyramid** of Giza
2 The **Hanging Gardens of Babylon**
3 The **Statue of Zeus** at Olympia
4 The **Temple of Artemis** in Ephesus
5 The **Mausoleum** of Maussolus
6 The **Colossus** of Rhodes
7 The **Pharos** of Alexandria

Mount Rushmore is located in South Dakota, USA. The faces of the four presidents: **George Washington, Thomas Jefferson, Theodore Roosevelt** and **Abraham Lincoln**, are <u>carved</u> into a <u>granite</u> mountain. The <u>monument</u> took 14 years to complete.

Mount Rushmore built 1927-1941

Golden Gate Bridge built 1930-1937

Empire State Building built 1930

Chichén Itzá, built 600-1400

Panama Canal, built 1914

Machu Picchu, built 1440-1532

Statue of Christ the Redeemer, built 1931

The **Colossus of Rhodes** was a huge <u>bronze statue</u> that stood at the harbour on Rhodes. It was 33 metres high and represented the sun god Helios. It is said to have taken twelve years to construct. What it looked like and exactly where it stood are not known for certain. In the Middle Ages it was believed that it stood with one foot on each side of the harbour entrance, so that boats had to sail under the statue, but this is probably incorrect.

MODERN WONDERS

- Chichén Itzá
- The Empire State Building
- The Golden Gate Bridge
- Machu Picchu
- Mount Rushmore
- The Panama Canal
- Statue of Christ the Redeemer

OTHER FAMOUS WONDERS

Stonehenge

Colosseum

<u>Catacombs</u> of Kom El Shoqafa

Great Wall of China

Porcelain Tower of Nanjing

Taj Mahal

Leaning Tower of Pisa

Hagia Sophia church

Petra

<u>Terracotta</u> Warriors

800 BC	500 AD	1500 AD
Antiquity	**The Middle Ages**	**Modern times**

! The **Statue of Zeus at Olympia** in Greece stood at the place that gave its name to the Olympic Games. The Games were held to honour the god Zeus. The statue was as tall as a four-storey building, 13 metres. It was destroyed in a fire in 462.

The Statue of Zeus at Olympia

Mausoleum of Halicarnassus

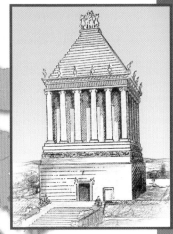

The remnants of the **Temple of Artemis** in **ancient** Ephesus in Turkey, considered to be the most beautiful building ever built. The temple was begun in 541 BC and was burned down two hundred years later.

Stonehenge

Colosseum Hagia Sophia Church

Great Wall of China

⊙ The **Mausoleum of Halicarnassus** is located near Bodrum in Turkey. A beautifully **decorated** tomb was built for King Mausolos.

Leaning Tower of Pisa

⚑ Construction of the **Colossus of Rhodes** began in 292 BC. The 33-metre high shining bronze statue stood at the harbour entrance on the island of Rhodes in the Mediterranean. The Colossus was destroyed 56 years later in an **earthquake**.

Petra

Taj Mahal

Terracotta Warriors Porcelain Tower of Nanjing

Catacombs of Kom El Shoqafa

! If the **Hanging Gardens of Babylon** had actually existed, they would have been located somewhere south of Baghdad in Iraq. They were **exotic** gardens that, according to **poets** and Greek **historians,** existed more than a thousand years ago.

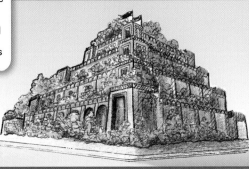

The Hanging Gardens of Babylon

⊙ The **Lighthouse** (or **Pharos**) of **Alexandria** was a practical wonder. It was completely destroyed by an **earthquake** in 1323, and parts of the **lighthouse** were used to build a mediaeval fort now standing on the same site.

⊙ The **Great Pyramid of Giza** in Egypt is the only one of the ancient **wonders** still in existence. The pyramid was built in 2560 BC as a **tomb**. It took around 20 years to build and was 146 metres high.

! The word **pharos** is the origin of the word for lighthouse in French, Spanish and Italian.

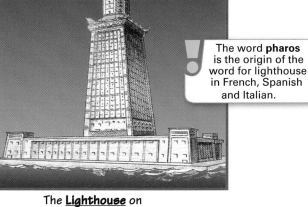

The **Lighthouse** on Pharos

The Great Pyramid of Giza

Tallest BUILDINGS

1	CN Tower	Toronto, Canada
2	Sears Tower	Chicago, USA
3	Taipei Tower	Taipei, Taiwan
4	Petronas Towers	Kuala Lumpur, Malaysia
5	Empire State Building	New York, USA
6	Jin Mao Building	Shanghai, China
7	Two International	Hong Kong, China
8	CITIC Plaza	Guanchou, China
9	Shun Hing Square	Shenzen, China
10	Central Plaza	Hong Kong, China

The Sears Tower has 102 lifts in all. Some of these offer the longest and fastest lift rides in the world.

The CN Tower is the tallest tower in the world. On 27 July 1979, Patrick Bailie dropped an egg from a height of 341 metres without it breaking.

It is not easy to determine which building is the tallest. It depends whether you include all masts, <u>antennas</u> or <u>spires</u> that may be present on the top of tall buildings. Our list includes all such objects. Sometimes **buildings** that do not contain homes or offices are discounted, but we have included some of these in our list.

There are also tall TV or radio masts that are simply straight poles. The tallest of these is in the city of Fargo, USA, and is 628 metres tall.

The **Empire State Building** also has a tall spire on the top. This was originally to have been used for anchoring <u>hot-air balloons</u>.

Some tall buildings

metres

600

500

400

300

200

100

0

CN (Canadian National) Tower, Toronto, Canada
built 1976
with antenna 553 m
roof 457 m
157 floors

Sears Tower,
Chicago, USA
built 1974
antenna 527 m
roof 442 m
108 floors

Taipei Tower,
Taipei, Taiwan
built 2004
antenna 508 m
roof 448 m
101 floors

Petronas
Twin Towers,
Kuala Lumpur,
Malaysia
built 1998
spire 452 m
roof 378 m
88 floors

Empire State Building,
New York, USA
built 1931
antenna 449 m
roof 381 m
102 floors

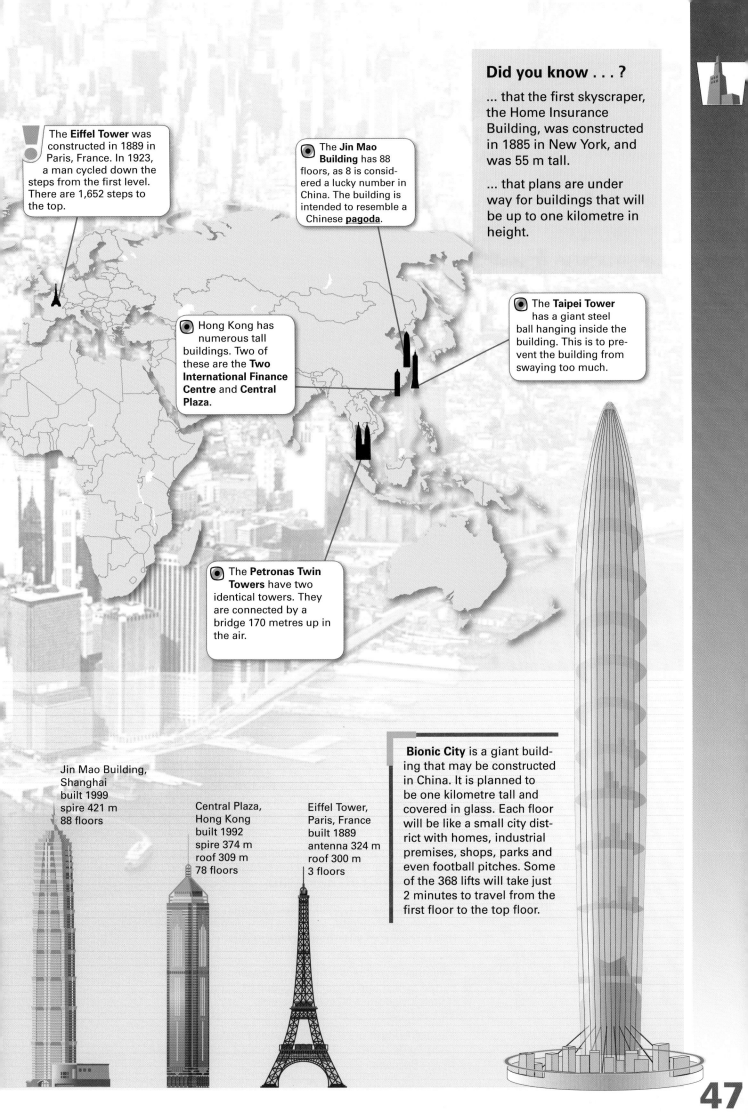

The **Eiffel Tower** was constructed in 1889 in Paris, France. In 1923, a man cycled down the steps from the first level. There are 1,652 steps to the top.

The **Jin Mao Building** has 88 floors, as 8 is considered a lucky number in China. The building is intended to resemble a Chinese **pagoda**.

Hong Kong has numerous tall buildings. Two of these are the **Two International Finance Centre** and **Central Plaza**.

The **Taipei Tower** has a giant steel ball hanging inside the building. This is to prevent the building from swaying too much.

The **Petronas Twin Towers** have two identical towers. They are connected by a bridge 170 metres up in the air.

Bionic City is a giant building that may be constructed in China. It is planned to be one kilometre tall and covered in glass. Each floor will be like a small city district with homes, industrial premises, shops, parks and even football pitches. Some of the 368 lifts will take just 2 minutes to travel from the first floor to the top floor.

Jin Mao Building, Shanghai
built 1999
spire 421 m
88 floors

Central Plaza, Hong Kong
built 1992
spire 374 m
roof 309 m
78 floors

Eiffel Tower, Paris, France
built 1889
antenna 324 m
roof 300 m
3 floors

47

The longest SUSPENSION BRIDGES

1	Akashi Kaikyo Bridge	Japan	1,990 m
2	Great Belt Bridge	Danmark	1,624 m
3	Runyang Bridge	China	1,490 m
4	Humber Bridge	England	1,410 m
5	Jiangyin Bridge	China	1,385 m
6	Tsing Ma Bridge	Hong Kong	1,377 m
7	Verrazano Narrows	USA	1,298 m
8	Golden Gate Bridge	USA	1,280 m
9	High Coast Bridge	Sweden	1,210 m
10	Mackinac Bridge	USA	1,158 m

m=metres

The **Forth Rail Bridge** in Scotland is a bridge-building **masterpiece**, built in 1890. It takes 3 years to paint, and once the painters reach the end it's time to go back and start again!

NORTH AMERICA

Golden Gate Bridge

Pontchartrain Causeway

Verrazano Narrows Bridge

SOUTH AMERICA

The **Verrazano Narrows Bridge** is in New York and connects Brooklyn and Staten Island. In summer the **roadway** is 4 metres longer than in winter – as the bridge expands when it's hot.

The **Golden Gate Bridge** at the **en-trance** to San Francisco Bay was completed in 1937. It is painted a well-known shade of red. During construction a **safety net** was hung underneath the bridge, and saved the lives of 19 workers.

The **Pontchartrain Causeway** in Louisiana, USA, is the world's longest **girder bridge**. It is 38.4 kilometres long.

Different types of bridges

Suspension bridges are called that because the bridge deck is suspended from long **cables** secured to high towers. It is this type of bridge that can have the longest distance or span between the towers.

A **cable-stayed bridge** is a girder bridge strengthened by inclined **cables**. The **Öresund Bridge** is an example of this kind of bridge and is one of the few with **carriageways** for both cars and trains.

Girder bridges are generally bridges made of **steel** and **concrete**. Europe's longest girder bridge is the Öland Bridge, which is 6,072 metres long.

Arch bridges are a type of bridge generally made of **steel** or **reinforced concrete**. The most famous bridge of this type is the **Sydney Harbour Bridge** in Australia.

A **cantilever bridge** is a bridge with several **beams** supported by a single pillar. The Forth Rail Bridge in the United Kingdom is a classic example.

Vaulted bridges are the oldest type of bridge and are often made of stone. This type of bridge was even used by the **Romans**.

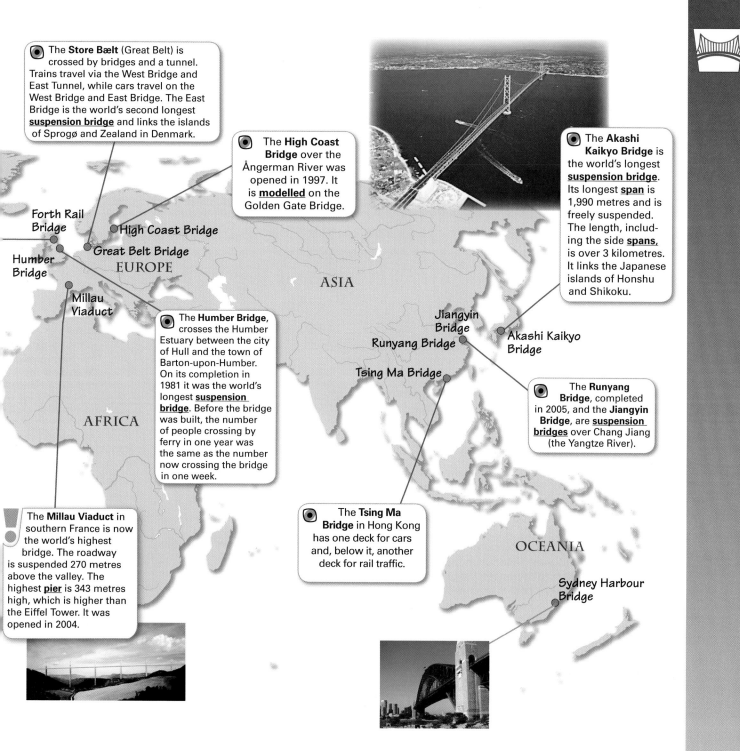

The **Store Bælt** (Great Belt) is crossed by bridges and a tunnel. Trains travel via the West Bridge and East Tunnel, while cars travel on the West Bridge and East Bridge. The East Bridge is the world's second longest **suspension bridge** and links the islands of Sprogø and Zealand in Denmark.

The **High Coast Bridge** over the Ångerman River was opened in 1997. It is **modelled** on the Golden Gate Bridge.

The **Akashi Kaikyo Bridge** is the world's longest **suspension bridge**. Its longest **span** is 1,990 metres and is freely suspended. The length, including the side **spans**, is over 3 kilometres. It links the Japanese islands of Honshu and Shikoku.

Forth Rail Bridge

High Coast Bridge

Great Belt Bridge

Humber Bridge

EUROPE

ASIA

Millau Viaduct

The **Humber Bridge**, crosses the Humber Estuary between the city of Hull and the town of Barton-upon-Humber. On its completion in 1981 it was the world's longest **suspension bridge**. Before the bridge was built, the number of people crossing by ferry in one year was the same as the number now crossing the bridge in one week.

AFRICA

Jiangyin Bridge

Runyang Bridge

Akashi Kaikyo Bridge

Tsing Ma Bridge

The **Runyang Bridge**, completed in 2005, and the **Jiangyin Bridge**, are **suspension bridges** over Chang Jiang (the Yangtze River).

The **Millau Viaduct** in southern France is now the world's highest bridge. The roadway is suspended 270 metres above the valley. The highest **pier** is 343 metres high, which is higher than the Eiffel Tower. It was opened in 2004.

The **Tsing Ma Bridge** in Hong Kong has one deck for cars and, below it, another deck for rail traffic.

OCEANIA

Sydney Harbour Bridge

You can only walk across **suspension bridges** like this. This type of bridge used to be constructed from **lianas**, ropes and wooden planks, just like you see in the Indiana Jones films.

Did you know . . . ?

... that a water bridge is known as an **aqueduct**. It can be used to transport fresh water or water for irrigation of crops or even for travelling by boat.

... that the longest cycle bridge is near the railway station in Cambridge, UK, and is 237 metres long.

... that the longest **steel** arch bridge is called Lupu Bridge and is located in Shanghai. It has a **span** of 550 metres.

... that there are plans to construct a bridge between Europe and Africa.

The Longest CANALS

1	**Saint Lawrence Seaway,** Canada/USA	3,780 km
2	**Rhine–Main–Danube Canal,** Germany	3,500 km
3	**Atlantic Intracoastal Waterway,** USA	3,000 km
4	**Gulf Intracoastal Waterway,** USA	2,080 km
5	**The Grand Canal,** China	1,790 km
6	**Belomor Canal,** Russia	504 km
7	**Canal du Midi,** France	241 km
8	**Göta Canal,** Sweden	190 km
9	**Suez Canal,** Egypt	163 km
10	**Casiquiares Canal,** Venezuela	163 km

The **Saint Lawrence Canal** runs from the Atlantic to the Great Lakes and is made up of several canals. Construction began on parts of this **waterway** back in the 1600s, but it was not possible for large **ocean-going vessels** to navigate the entire canal until the 1930s.

Canals have been constructed for both travelling by boat and transporting water. The information on these pages is about the longest canals and **canal systems** that are used for boat travel.

Locks are used to transfer boats vertically. The boat enters a **lock chamber** and is raised or lowered by closing the gates at one end and opening the gates at the other end, letting the water in or out. There are often several locks in a row.

There are also **boat lifts** that function like an ordinary lift. The boat enters a water-filled compartment. The entire compartment is then transferred to the higher or lower level, where the boat then continues on its journey.

NORTH AMERICA

The **Atlantic Intracoastal Waterway** from Virginia to Florida on the east coast of the USA was constructed for **goods transport**, but is now used mostly by **pleasure craft**.

The **Gulf Intracoastal Waterway** in the southern USA was completed during the Second World War and used by the American **military** to avoid German **u-boat attacks** in the Gulf of Mexico.

SOUTH AMERICA

Atlantic Ocean
● Colon
Panama Canal
Panama ●
Pacific Ocean

The **Panama Canal** Construction of this canal began in 1889 and took 25 years. It connects the Atlantic with the Pacific, so that vessels don't need to travel south round South America. Travelling through the canal takes approximately 10 hours.

Did you know . . . ?

... that the busiest canal in the world is the Kiel Canal, also called the **Nord-Ostsee Canal**.

... that the Suez Canal was closed between 1967 and 1975, following the war between Israel and the **Arab States**.

... that 13,000 vessels pass through the Panama Canal every year, but 48 is the maximum number that can pass through in one **day**.

... that the **Alentejo canals** in southern Portugal are approximately 9,000 km long, but are mostly used as **irrigation canals**. Construction began in 1959.

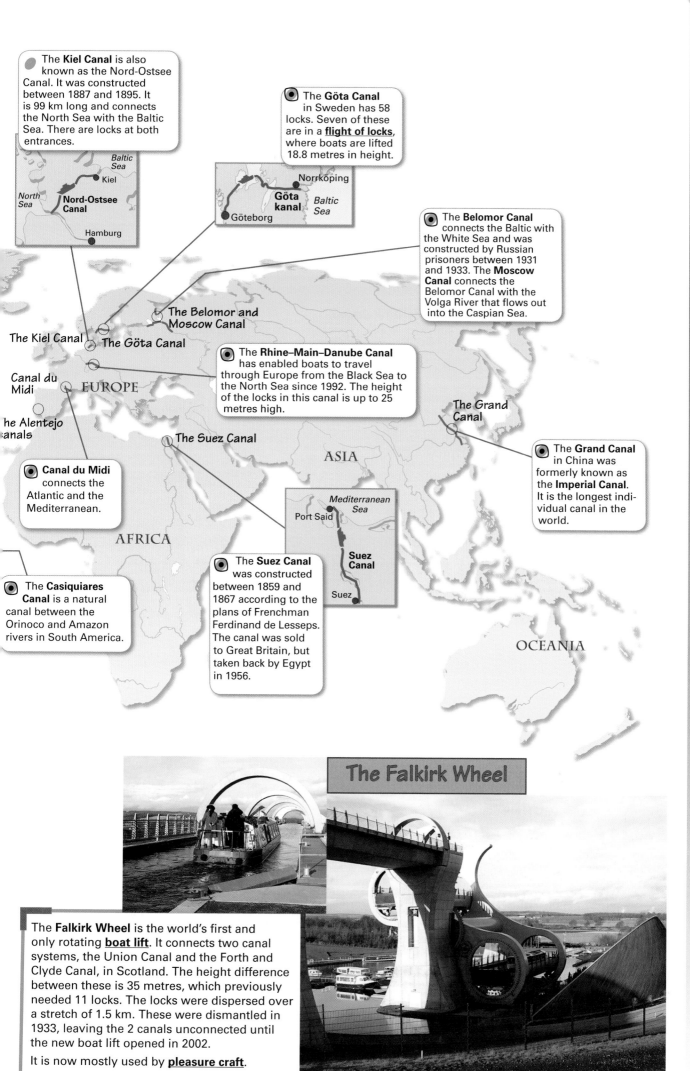

The **Kiel Canal** is also known as the Nord-Ostsee Canal. It was constructed between 1887 and 1895. It is 99 km long and connects the North Sea with the Baltic Sea. There are locks at both entrances.

Baltic Sea
Kiel
North Sea
Nord-Ostsee Canal
Hamburg

The **Göta Canal** in Sweden has 58 locks. Seven of these are in a **flight of locks**, where boats are lifted 18.8 metres in height.

Norrköping
Göta kanal
Baltic Sea
Göteborg

The **Belomor Canal** connects the Baltic with the White Sea and was constructed by Russian prisoners between 1931 and 1933. The **Moscow Canal** connects the Belomor Canal with the Volga River that flows out into the Caspian Sea.

The Belomor and Moscow Canal

The Kiel Canal
The Göta Canal

The **Rhine–Main–Danube Canal** has enabled boats to travel through Europe from the Black Sea to the North Sea since 1992. The height of the locks in this canal is up to 25 metres high.

The Grand Canal

Canal du Midi
EUROPE

he Alentejo anals

The Suez Canal

ASIA

The **Grand Canal** in China was formerly known as the **Imperial Canal**. It is the longest individual canal in the world.

Canal du Midi connects the Atlantic and the Mediterranean.

AFRICA

Mediterranean Sea
Port Said
Suez Canal
Suez

The **Casiquiares Canal** is a natural canal between the Orinoco and Amazon rivers in South America.

The **Suez Canal** was constructed between 1859 and 1867 according to the plans of Frenchman Ferdinand de Lesseps. The canal was sold to Great Britain, but taken back by Egypt in 1956.

OCEANIA

The Falkirk Wheel

The **Falkirk Wheel** is the world's first and only rotating **boat lift**. It connects two canal systems, the Union Canal and the Forth and Clyde Canal, in Scotland. The height difference between these is 35 metres, which previously needed 11 locks. The locks were dispersed over a stretch of 1.5 km. These were dismantled in 1933, leaving the 2 canals unconnected until the new boat lift opened in 2002.

It is now mostly used by **pleasure craft**.

The Longest TUNNELS

1	Seikan Tunnel	Tsugaru Strait, Japan	53.9 km
2	Eurotunnel	The English Channel	50 km
3	Iwate Ichinohe Tunnel	Tanigawa Mountains, Japan	25.8 km
4	Lærdal Tunnel	Norway	24.5 km
5	Dai Shimizu Tunnel	Mikuni Mountain Range, Japan	22.2 km
6	Simplon Tunnel	The Swiss Alps	19.8 km
7	Vereina Tunnel	Klosters-Sagliains, Switzerland	19.1 km
8	Shin Kanmon Tunnel	Kanmon Straits, Japan	18.7 km
9	Apennine Tunnel	Bologna-Florence, Italy	18.5 km
10	Qinling Tunnel	Qinling Mountains, China	18.5 km

Of the 10 longest tunnels in the world, only one is a **road tunnel** and the other nine are **railway tunnels**. Most are in Japan or Europe.

The **Seikan Tunnel** is the longest tunnel in the world. It runs under the water between the Japanese islands of Honshu and Hokkaido. It is 54 kilometres long. When a **typhoon** (tropical tornado) caused the deaths of over 1,400 people in boats travelling between the islands in 1954, the decision was made to commence building a tunnel.

The **Eurotunnel** is 50 kilometres long and runs under the English Channel between France and the UK. It is a **railway tunnel**.

If you want to take your car with you, there are special carriages where you can drive your car onto the train. The train can take up to 200 cars.

The **Eurotunnel** **connects** the United Kingdom with France and the rest of Europe.

NORTH AMERICA

The Big Dig

There are not many long tunnels in America, but one of the largest tunnel construction projects is in Boston, where they are planning to construct tunnels for cars, trains and the subway under the entire **city centre**. The **project** is known as "**The Big Dig**".

SOUTH AMERICA

La Galera

The highest tunnel in South America is at La Galera in Peru. It is 4,781 metres above sea level.

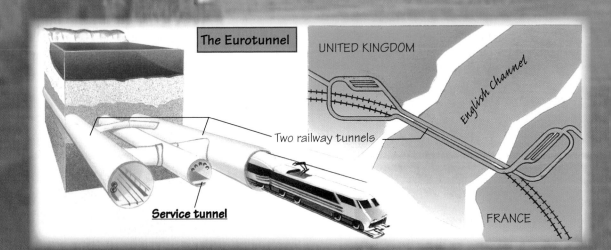

The Eurotunnel — UNITED KINGDOM — English Channel — Two railway tunnels — Service tunnel — FRANCE

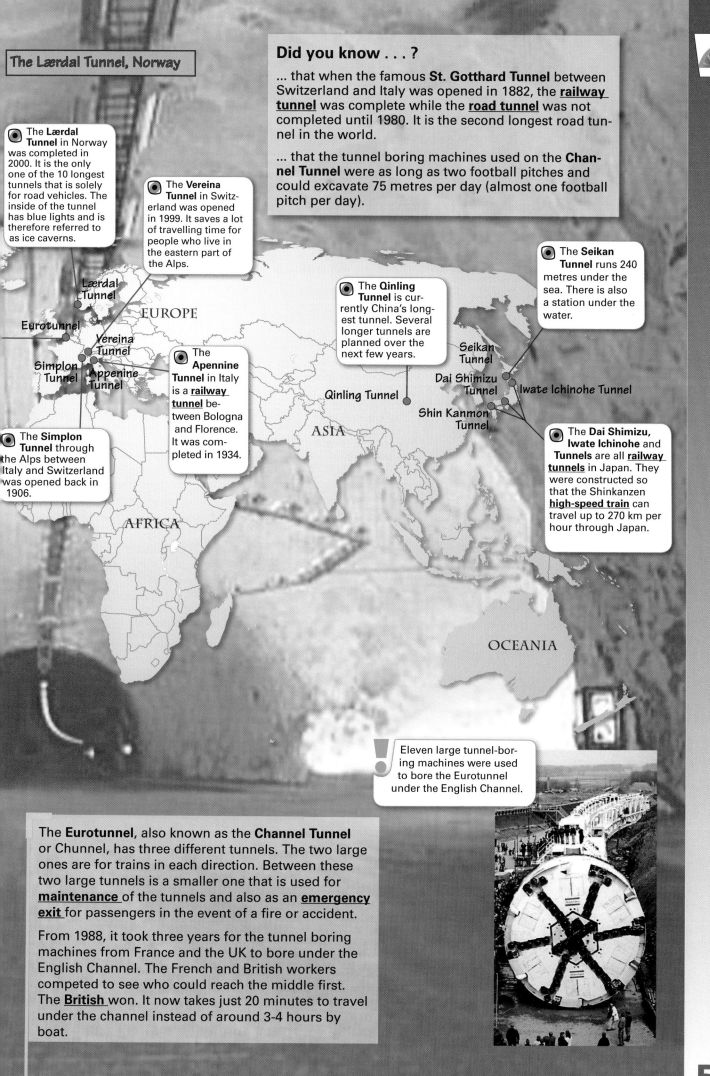

Did you know . . . ?

... that when the famous **St. Gotthard Tunnel** between Switzerland and Italy was opened in 1882, the **railway tunnel** was complete while the **road tunnel** was not completed until 1980. It is the second longest road tunnel in the world.

... that the tunnel boring machines used on the **Channel Tunnel** were as long as two football pitches and could excavate 75 metres per day (almost one football pitch per day).

The **Lærdal Tunnel** in Norway was completed in 2000. It is the only one of the 10 longest tunnels that is solely for road vehicles. The inside of the tunnel has blue lights and is therefore referred to as ice caverns.

The **Vereina Tunnel** in Switzerland was opened in 1999. It saves a lot of travelling time for people who live in the eastern part of the Alps.

The **Seikan Tunnel** runs 240 metres under the sea. There is also a station under the water.

The **Qinling Tunnel** is currently China's longest tunnel. Several longer tunnels are planned over the next few years.

The **Apennine Tunnel** in Italy is a **railway tunnel** between Bologna and Florence. It was completed in 1934.

The **Simplon Tunnel** through the Alps between Italy and Switzerland was opened back in 1906.

The **Dai Shimizu, Iwate Ichinohe** and **Tunnels** are all **railway tunnels** in Japan. They were constructed so that the Shinkanzen **high-speed train** can travel up to 270 km per hour through Japan.

EUROPE

Lærdal Tunnel

Eurotunnel

Vereina Tunnel

Simplon Tunnel

Appenine Tunnel

Qinling Tunnel

Seikan Tunnel

Dai Shimizu Tunnel

Iwate Ichinohe Tunnel

Shin Kanmon Tunnel

ASIA

AFRICA

OCEANIA

Eleven large tunnel-boring machines were used to bore the Eurotunnel under the English Channel.

The **Eurotunnel**, also known as the **Channel Tunnel** or Chunnel, has three different tunnels. The two large ones are for trains in each direction. Between these two large tunnels is a smaller one that is used for **maintenance** of the tunnels and also as an **emergency exit** for passengers in the event of a fire or accident.

From 1988, it took three years for the tunnel boring machines from France and the UK to bore under the English Channel. The French and British workers competed to see who could reach the middle first. The **British** won. It now takes just 20 minutes to travel under the channel instead of around 3-4 hours by boat.

The largest AIRPORTS

			passengers
1	Atlanta, Hartsfield	USA	79 million
2	Chicago, O'Hare	USA	69 million
3	London, Heathrow	Great Britain	63 million
4	Tokyo, Haneda	Japan	62 million
5	Los Angeles	USA	55 million
6	Dallas-Fort Worth	USA	53 million
7	Frankfurt am Main	Germany	48 million
8	Paris, Charles de Gaulle	France	48 million
9	Amsterdam, Schiphol	Netherlands	40 million
10	Denver	USA	37 million

The **Boeing 747** or Jumbo Jet is the most common plane for long journeys. It can take 375 passengers. Planes are now being built that can take up to 800 passengers.

At Chicago's large airport, **O'Hare**, 100 planes can take off and 100 planes land every hour.

Five of the ten largest airports in the world are in the USA. The USA is a large country, and therefore many people fly both within the USA and to other countries.

Hartsfield airport in Atlanta is the largest in the world. The airport has 146 gates for flights within the USA and 28 for **international** departures. Coca-Cola's head office is located in the city of Atlanta.

O'Hare airport in Chicago is named after an American soldier. He received the Navy's highest honour for his **heroic actions** during the Second World War.

Heathrow in London was already a **military** airfield during the First World War. After the end of the Second World War in 1946, it became an airport for ordinary **passengers**. The longest runway at Heathrow is almost 4 kilometres long.

Denver airport is used for travelling on to many of the ski resorts in the Rocky Mountains.

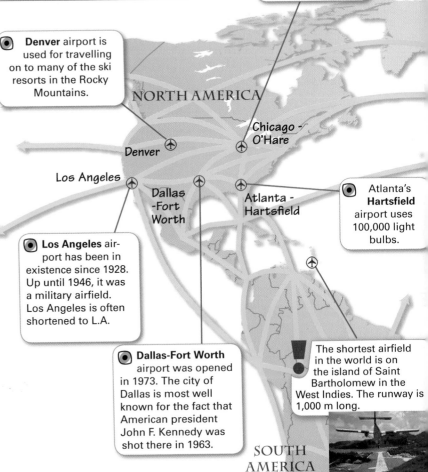

NORTH AMERICA

Denver

Chicago - O'Hare

Los Angeles

Dallas -Fort Worth

Atlanta - Hartsfield

Atlanta's **Hartsfield** airport uses 100,000 light bulbs.

Los Angeles airport has been in existence since 1928. Up until 1946, it was a military airfield. Los Angeles is often shortened to L.A.

Dallas-Fort Worth airport was opened in 1973. The city of Dallas is most well known for the fact that American president John F. Kennedy was shot there in 1963.

The shortest airfield in the world is on the island of Saint Bartholomew in the West Indies. The runway is 1,000 m long.

SOUTH AMERICA

A great number of planes take off and land at airports every day. A ve[ry] well-organised system is needed in the air and on the ground to ensu[re] that no planes crash. When planes approach an airport they must wai[t] in the air at different heights, "stacking", until it is their turn to land. T[he] **air traffic control tower** at an airport **controls** each plane in its radar s[ys]-tems. The tower gives instructions to each plane about where it shou[ld] fly, when it should land or taxi on the ground.

Did you know . . . ?

... that the **Wright Brothers'** plane was the first that could fly. That was in 1903, and the flight lasted 12 seconds.

... that the first person to fly across the English Channel was Frenchman **Bleriot** in 1909. It took 37 minutes.

... that the first person to fly across the Atlantic was **Charles Lindberg**, a Swedish **descendant**. On 20 May 1927, he took off from New York's airfield and landed 33 hours, 30 minutes and 29.8 seconds later outside Paris.

... that the fastest flight across the Atlantic from New York to London took 2 hours 52 minutes and 59 seconds. That was by a **Concorde aircraft** in 1990.

... that New York was the first airport to have long corridors out to the runways, so that **passengers** didn't have to go outside to board planes.

... that a Boeing 747 uses just as much **fuel** to fly from London to Hong Kong as a car would use to drive around the world 40 times.

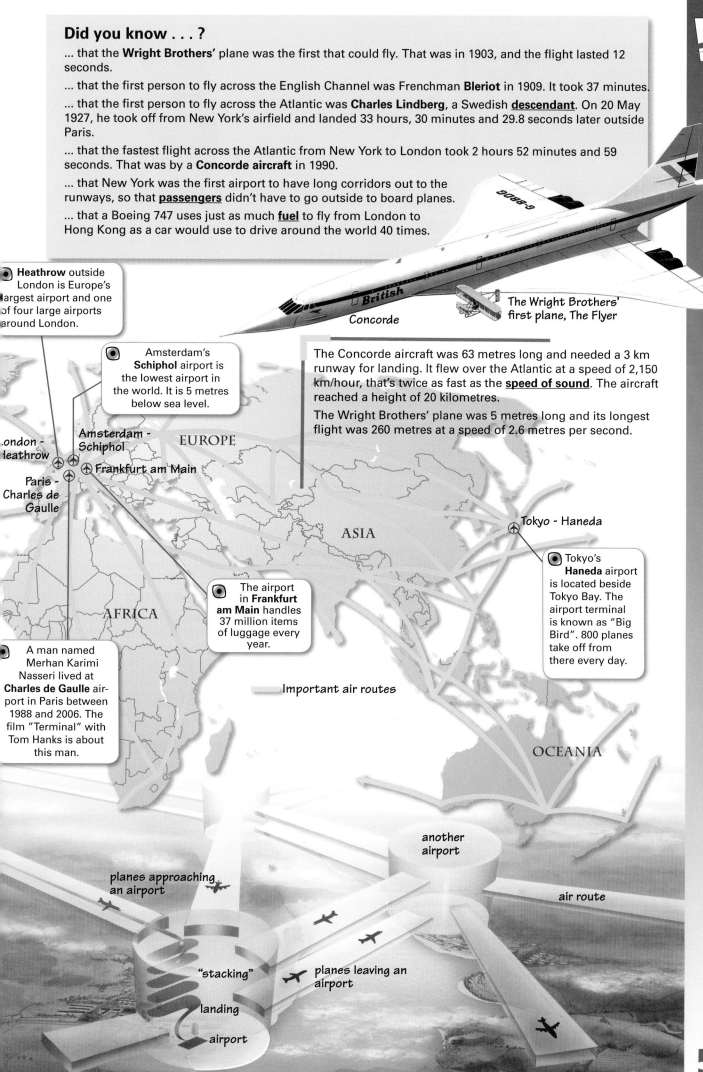

Concorde

The Wright Brothers' first plane, The Flyer

Heathrow outside London is Europe's largest airport and one of four large airports around London.

Amsterdam's **Schiphol** airport is the lowest airport in the world. It is 5 metres below sea level.

The Concorde aircraft was 63 metres long and needed a 3 km runway for landing. It flew over the Atlantic at a speed of 2,150 km/hour, that's twice as fast as the **speed of sound**. The aircraft reached a height of 20 kilometres.

The Wright Brothers' plane was 5 metres long and its longest flight was 260 metres at a speed of 2.6 metres per second.

London - Heathrow

Amsterdam - Schiphol

EUROPE

Paris - Charles de Gaulle

Frankfurt am Main

ASIA

Tokyo - Haneda

Tokyo's **Haneda** airport is located beside Tokyo Bay. The airport terminal is known as "Big Bird". 800 planes take off from there every day.

The airport in **Frankfurt am Main** handles 37 million items of luggage every year.

AFRICA

A man named Merhan Karimi Nasseri lived at **Charles de Gaulle** airport in Paris between 1988 and 2006. The film "Terminal" with Tom Hanks is about this man.

Important air routes

OCEANIA

another airport

planes approaching an airport

air route

"stacking"

planes leaving an airport

landing

airport

EXPLANATION OF WORDS

Here are some words that you may be wondering about

Some of the words explained here can have several different meanings. The explanations only tell you what the words mean in this book.

A

aborigine

a member of the people who are the oldest known inhabitants of a particular area

Aborigines

original inhabitants of Australia

accounts

notes on a person's money resources

adventurer

person who does exciting and dangerous things

air traffic control tower

where plane movements are controlled

alphabet

the letters of a language in a fixed order; comes from the names of the first two Greek letters, alfa and beta

American

person from America or the USA

ancient

old or something belonging to the time period Antiquity (see the time chart on page 44)

anorak

a jacket with a hood, originally from Greenland

antenna

a tall metallic object that can receive radio signals

anthozoa

creatures such as corals, sea anemones, etc. that live in warm oceans

aqueduct

water bridge carrying a canal over a road

Arab states

states with Arabic-speaking inhabitants and with Arabic cultures; generally refers to states in North Africa, the Middle East and the Arabian Peninsula

arctic

something in the area around the North Pole

area

size or area of a region

atmosphere

layer of gas around the Earth

avenue

wide street, often lined with trees

B

ballooning

flying by air balloon that generally contains hot air; cannot be steered but is carried by the wind

Bantu

group of approximately 500 languages spoken in Africa; the most well known is Swahili

bathyscaphe

underwater craft that can travel down to great depths and consists of a pressure chamber with a window; it cannot move sideways

Beaufort

scale for showing wind speed

bird of prey

bird that eats other animals, has sharp claws and a sharp beak

boat/ship lift

device for moving vessels vertically

boomerang

a curved throwing stick that is used for both sport and hunting; it is thrown into the wind and if it does not hit its target, it will return to the thrower

boomerang

breeder

person who breeds animals

bristlecone pine

pine species that can live to be very old; it has needles in groups of five; found in the USA

British

person who comes from Great Britain

bronze statue

statue made of bronze (which is generally a mixture of copper and tin)

Bushmen

people also known as San, who live in the Kalahari in southern Africa and speak the Khoisan language

C

cable

can be made of rope and thread or steel

cable-stayed bridge

girder bridge that is also suspended by cables so that it can cope with heavy loads; the longest example in Sweden is the Uddevalla Bridge

canal

man-made waterway for traffic or irrigation

canal system

several connected canals; may also pass through lakes and rivers

capital city

the location of the government and parliament, often a large city but not always the largest in the country; often shown on maps in capital letters or underlined

caribou

an Indian name for the North American type of reindeer

carriageway

section of a road that is for driving motor vehicles

carve

to make a figure out of stone, clay or wood

caste

divided classes in Indian society

catacombs

underground burial site

celsius

unit of temperature, named after Swede Anders Celsius. Zero degrees is equivalent to the melting point of ice and 100 degrees is the boiling point of water

chinook

dry, warm wind that blows on the eastern side of the Rocky Mountains, but also the name of an Indian nation

city centre

old central section of a city

city district

area with a distinct appearance, population or use within a city

coelacanth

fish that has fins that resemble brushes; thought to be extinct, but lives at great depths and is a predatory fish

colony

populated area that is governed by a country other than those who originally lived there

colossus

giant statue

concrete

a mixture of stone, cement and water; one of the most common materials in buildings

coniferous forest

forest made up of conifers; heather, bilberries, lingonberries, mosses and lichens often grow under the trees

connect

to link two points together

continent

continuous land mass. There are reckoned to be 7 continents: Africa, Antarctica, Asia, Australia, Europe, North America and South America

continental shelf

the flat section in the ocean closest to the coast, as much as around 200 metres deep, until the steep continental slope begins and the ocean becomes even deeper

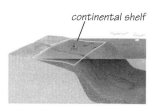

continental shelf

control

to supervise

coral reef

rock-like structure made of skeletons of anthozoa, found in tropical oceans where the water temperature is above 20 degrees

cotton plantation

area where cotton shrubs are grown to extract cotton from their fruit; grows in hot areas around the world

cycle

constant movement of substances in nature, e.g. water

cyclone

tornado or typhoon, spiral wind

D

D.C.

District of Columbia; this abbreviation is used when you mean the capital of the USA, Washington DC, as there is also a state called Washington

dam

structure that dams up water in an artificial lake

day

24 hours, a night and a day; the time it takes for the Earth to rotate once

deciduous forest

forest made up of deciduous trees that generally lose their leaves, but can also include trees that keep their leaves all year; the most common Swedish deciduous trees are aspen, birch, oak, lime and maple

decorate

to ornament

delta

deposit at the mouth of a river

densely populated

where many people live in a small area

descendant

person who is a younger relative in a family or social group

dinosaur

large extinct reptile

dissolution

cease to be a whole

doctor

strong wind that blows along the coast of South Africa

dominate

to be the most prominent

dromedary

a camel with one hump; a tame animal suited to living in desert areas; can close its nostrils when sand is blowing, has long eyelashes and can go without water for long periods

drop

the height difference in a water course

dry season

period when there is no rain

E

Earth's crust

the Earth's outer layer that is 35-50 km thick under the continents and 5-15 km under the oceans

earthquake

vibrations in the Earth's crust that cause cracks or faults to form and the ground to vibrate; can cause great destruction

ebb

falling water or low water in connection with the tide; generally occurs twice per day

electricity

strong form of energy, which can drive engines and appliances; also referred to as power

emergency exit

extra exit to be used in an emergency

endangered

risk that the species will die out

environment

region with specific conditions

equator

the "waist" of the Earth, imaginary line around the thickest point of the Earth

Eskimo

person from Greenland, also known as Inuit

Eucalyptus tree

tree originally from Australia that grows quickly and consumes a lot of water; eucalyptus oil, which is used for throat lozenges, can be obtained from this tree

evaporate

when a liquid changes into a gas; to disappear

exotic

foreign, from a distant country

explorer

person whose job is to travel into unexplored areas

extraction

handling raw materials

extremely

very, excessively

F

film industry

filming, sales and releasing of films

flight of locks

several locks in a row; the lock gates can be used at both ends

flow

rising water or high water in connection with the tide; generally occurs twice per day; or water course

force of gravity

celestial bodies have a force to attract things; on Earth, things fall to the ground

four-footed

another term for four-legged

fresh water

water with a low salt content

fuel

material that provides energy

föhn wind

warm dry wind that blows down from higher heights

gas cylinder

a tank containing oxygen

geologist

person who works on the science of the structure of the Earth

giant sequoia

American coniferous tree; a cypress with small scaly needles; can grow up to 100 metres tall and live to 4,000 years old; is an endangered species

ginkgo

sometimes called temple tree and available as a garden plant; old species that is found in temple grounds in China and Japan

girder bridge

usually made of steel or re-inforced concrete, long girders up to 200 metres long can be used, the most common types of bridges in modern roads are girder bridges

glacier

hard-packed mass of snow and ice found in cold regions

goods transport

moving goods

government

the highest controlling body in a country

granite

type of rock that is often used for buildings and monuments, common rock in Sweden

groundwater

water found in earth layers or bedrock; lakes and rivers are formed where the water comes up to the surface

growing period

period when trees grow and produce flowers and leaves

H

hemisphere

division of the globe into two halves; sometimes divided into western and eastern so that North and South America are in the western half and the other continents in the eastern half, sometimes northern and southern, above and below the equator

heroic actions

something worthy of admiration

high-speed train

express train that travels at 200 kilometres per hour or faster

Hindus

name of indigenous Indians in both cultural and religious terms

historian

person who does research into history

hot-air balloon

air balloon containing hot air; cannot be steered but is carried by the wind

hurricane

very powerful tropical tornado

hydrophone

device for listening to sounds in water

I

iceberg

floating blocks of ice that have broken loose from glaciers; more ice is generally concealed below the surface of the water than is visible above

independent

a country that is not dependent on any other country, but controls and decides on everything within the actual country

Indian

original population of America, who came from Asia 20,000 years ago when Asia was connected to Alaska

industrial city

city with many factories producing goods

inhabitant

person who lives in a certain area

inland ice

thick ice sheet (generally 100 metres thick) on top of land and ocean in extremely cold places

international

concerning many countries

Inuit

Greenlandic word for people previously known as Eskimos

irrigation

watering the soil so that things will grow better

Islam

religion with Mohammed as its prophet and the Koran as its holy scripture

J

jellyfish

creature that lives in the ocean; has a gelatinous body with long tentacles, found in all oceans

jungle

dense tropical forest

K

Khoisan

southern Africa's original population; have also been known as Hottentots and Bushmen

L

lake

large pool of water, in contrast to ocean

liana/vine

climbing plant in tropical forests

lighthouse

light signal for navigating at sea

llama

a relative of the camel that is found in South America's mountain districts

lock

device that allows boats to be raised or lowered where there are height differences in waterways

lock chamber

rectangular basin

logging

felling of trees

M

maintenance

upkeep to ensure that something functions

mammal

animals that give birth to live young, suckle their young, breathe with lungs and have a developed brain

Maoris

original population of New Zealand

masterpiece

something skilfully made

mausoleum

large tomb

Middle East

geographical region between Europe and Asia; the term is generally used for the countries of Lebanon, Israel, Syria, Jordan, Iraq, Saudi Arabia, Kuwait and Iran, but Turkey is sometimes included too

military

fighting forces whose task is to protect a country

minority

smaller part, opposite of majority

mirage

can occur above snow surfaces, desert areas or asphalt surfaces; caused by the refraction of light rays, producing an optical illusion

missionary

person who is sent out to spread a religion

mistral

strong northerly wind in France

mixed forest

forest containing more than one species of tree; in Sweden, generally pine and spruce together with birch and aspen

model

something you try to imitate

Mongols

original population of Mongolia led by Ghengis Khan

monk

a man who is a member of a monastic order

monsoon forest

forest, primarily in southern Asia, where monsoon rain occurs in summer; has trees that lose their leaves

monument

memorial

mountain plateau

flat mountain region at a high level

mountain range

long region of mountains

mountaineer

person who dedicates themselves to climbing mountains, sometimes as an explorer and sometimes as a sport

mouth

entrance to a harbour, or where a river flows out into the sea

musk ox

protected hoofed animal with short legs and a long coat; can be up to 2.5 metres long and 1.2 metres tall

Muslim

follower of the religion of Islam

N

national flag

flag that is the symbol of a state

national park

area where the countryside and wildlife is protected

national register

information on where people live and their address

naval flag

special flags flown on warships and military buildings

nocturnal

nocturnal animals are animals that are active at night

nomads

people who live in desert areas and accompany their animals as they search for fresh pasture

North Pole

point where the Earth's axis intersects the surface of the Earth in the northern hemisphere

North Pole

nunatak

Greenlandic word for a peak of rock sticking up out of a glacier or inland ice

O

oasis

area in the desert where things can grow, as water can come up to the surface; there are natural and also man-made oases, where the water is pumped up

ocean trenches

also known as ocean deeps, found between the plates that form the Earth's crust

ocean wave

large waves in the ocean can be caused by both strong winds and earthquakes or volcanic eruptions on the ocean floor

ocean-going vessel

large vessel constructed for crossing the oceans with large loads

opposition

differing opinions and interests

orang utan

large ape species that can be up to 1.8 metres tall and weigh 90 kilos, has long arms and fingers; the males have large cheek pads

original population

the people who are the oldest known inhabitants of a particular area

oxygen

colourless and odourless gas, an element, present in air. Pure oxygen is used in gas cylinders when additional oxygen is required for breathing, e.g. for mountaineering and diving

P

pagoda

Asian tower structure divided into floors

palace

stately building for important people

pankration

martial art in the ancient Olympiads; kicking and punching was permitted to get your opponent to give up

parka

Greenlandic knee-length jacket with hood

passenger

person who travels in a vehicle but is not the driver

people

a group of people with a common appearance and a shared culture

pier

pillar that holds up a bridge

pillar

strong post often used in construction work

plankton

small plants and creatures that drift around in water and oceans

plantation owner

owner of a large plantation or estate

pleasure craft

boats used for leisure outings

poet

writer; person who writes poetry

polar explorer

person who works in research on nature and phenomena in the polar regions. Salomon August Andrée was a famous Swedish polar explorer who attempted to reach the North Pole by air balloon in 1897, but this ended with the death of Andrée and his two travelling companions at Spitsbergen

precipitation

water that falls to earth; can be liquid or solid in form, such as rain, snow, sleet or hail

predator

animal that lives on land and eats meat; often has sharp canine teeth and molars

predatory fish

fish that eat other fish, e.g. shark and pike

prehistoric

time when humans were around, but nothing was written down; the only things we know about this period come from finds from excavations

president

head of a republic, generally elected by the people

project

work or plan with a specific goal

pygmies

a people of short stature in Africa

radio communication

takes place through transfer of information via radio waves; you can hear speech via signals transmitted through the air

radius

straight line from the centre of a circle to its outer edge

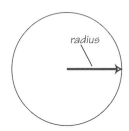

railway tunnel

tunnel built for trains

rainforest

forest in rainy areas where the trees do not lose their leaves; there are both tropical and temperate rainforests, depending on where on Earth they are located

rare

only occurs in small numbers

ravine

deep and narrow valley

reckless

person who is both daring and foolish

region

area or district

reinforced concrete

concrete that is strengthened with iron rods or mesh

relay

team event where several runners run a leg each

religion

belief in a higher power or god

research station

stations at locations in Antarctica where researchers live for varying periods, e.g. while taking measurements in the ice

rest period

the rest period for trees is when they lose their leaves and don't grow, resting instead

road tunnel

tunnel built for road vehicles

roadway

the part of a bridge where vehicles travel

rock desert

desert consisting of bare rock

rodent

mammal with long curved front teeth that have to keep growing throughout its life because they are constantly being worn down, e.g. squirrels, guinea pigs and rats

Roman

inhabitant of the Roman Empire

runes

the Germanic people's first form of writing, which used angular letters because they carved them in stone using a hammer and chisel

rush-hour

heavy traffic during periods when many people are travelling to or from work

S

safety net

net used to catch objects or people, suspended from places with a risk of accidents

salt desert

desert where the earth layer is salt after the salt water has evaporated

salt lagoon

shallow lake with salt water near the beach

salt lake

lake with salt water; often found in deserts where the water evaporates, leaving the salt behind

Sami

people in northern Scandinavia (previously known as Lapps) or language spoken by the Sami; different dialects exist: southern Sami and northern Sami

sand desert

desert consisting of sand, often has large sand dunes

sand dune

accumulation of sand piled up in one place by the wind

savannah

grassy region with shrubs and trees

seafarer

person who makes long sea journeys

service tunnel

tunnel used for repairing another tunnel or as an emergency exit, etc.

settled

people who live permanently in the same place, compare the opposite: nomads

settler

person who moves to an area that has been uninhabited or inhabited by other people

sheikh

Arab title for a head of a family or tribe

Siberian

from Siberia in northern Russia

silt
mud or clay water

sirocco
strong hot southerly wind from the Sahara carrying dust that blows in over Italy

situated
=is located

slave
a person who is someone else's property and must perform work as ordered

sloth
two or three-toed sloth with powerful legs, a short snout, and long hair; moves incredibly slowly

slum area
tumble-down residential area with flimsy buildings

snorkel
breathing tube used for swimming just under the surface of the water

snow-capped
covered in snow

soda lake
lake with a lot of soda and salt; insufficient water supply

solo expedition
journey that someone makes completely alone

South Pole
point where the Earth's axis intersects the surface of the Earth in the southern hemisphere

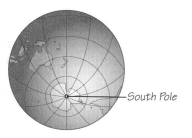
—South Pole

span
part of a bridge between two anchor points

speed of sound
sound travels through the air at a rate of around 1,000 kilometres per hour

spire
pointed roof on a building; resembles an antenna

state
province or part of a country; a state can have some self-government

steel
mixture of iron and a little carbon

stony desert
desert where the ground is covered by stones; the most common type of desert

sugar cane plantation
large plantation or estate where sugar cane is grown

Sumerians
people who lived between the Euphrates and Tigris rivers several thousand years BC in the region now known as Iraq

survey
to make a map of an area

suspension bridge
type of bridge where the actual carriageway is suspended from steel cables that are fastened to towers of steel or concrete; the only option for building bridges where there is a long gap to be crossed

symbol
character or figure that has a specific meaning

T

temple
religious building

terracotta
reddish-brown fired clay

Tibetans
people who speak Tibetan in Tibet, India, Bhutan and Nepal

tide
rises and falls in the surface of the ocean resulting from the gravity of the moon and sun; the differences are most marked in the English Channel and in Canada; see: ebb, flow

tomb
memorial and grave

Tonga
kingdom in the southern Pacific Ocean

torch
stick with flammable material that allows you to carry fire

tornado
cyclone

tradition
recurring event

transport
to move something from one place to another

tray
open container

tropical forest
forest found near the equator

tropical rainforest
rainforest that is constantly green, with different tree layers; found in areas near the equator

tsar
historical name of the ruler of Russia; emperor

tsunami
Japanese word for tidal wave used in numerous languages.

Tuareg
Muslims found in desert and steppe areas in Africa; nomads or sometimes farmers

turban

long length of cloth wound around the head; can be various colours and shapes

typhoon

tropical whirlwind in the Pacific, north of the equator, with a wind-force equivalent to a hurricane

U

u-boat attack

attacks against ships by a sub-marine under the water

underwater craft

vehicle used for research under-water; could be a submarine or a bathyscaphe

UNESCO

United Nations Educational, Scientific and Cultural Organization, a body within the United Nations (UN) that works towards collaboration within edu-cation, science and culture

uninhabited

area where no-one lives

union

an alliance for a specific purpose

university

institute for education after sec-ondary school and for research

V

volcanic eruption

when a volcano erupts, magma comes up to the surface through cracks in the Earth's crust; the magma solidifies in time and is known as lava

volcano

point where hot magma (lava) forces its way up from inside the Earth

voyages of discovery

journeys made to explore new areas

W

waterway

connections between bodies of water via canals, rivers and lakes

willy-willy

tropical whirlwind in south-western Australia

wind-force

measured on a scale using a sys-tem known as Beaufort (see page 20), which can be converted into wind speed measured in metres per second

wingspan

width of a bird's outstretched wings from one wing tip to the other

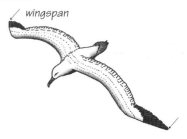

wipe out

to put an end to; exterminate

wonder

something unbelievable

working day

portion of a day that people work

world heritage

natural or cultural heritage that is important to preserve

written characters

letters, numbers and various symbols

Y

yeti

abominable snowman in Tibet, who leaves footprints in the snow

*Students from Bournemouth University in the UK hold the record for
the maximum number of a people in a Volkswagen.
103 people travelled 4.5 metres.*

LOOKING FOR A SPECIAL WORD?

Here are some vocabulary words and the pages where you can find out more about them.

One of the last large steam engines of the Challenger series in North America that were constructed for rapidly transporting goods and passengers from the eastern USA to California and the west coast.